L O V E
W R I T I N G

SUE MOORCROFT

Published by Accent Press Ltd – 2010

ISBN 9781906373993

Copyright © Sue Moorcroft 2010

Printed and bound in the UK
by CPI Bookmarque, Croydon, CR0 4TD

Cover design by Red Dot Design

For the many contributors to this book.

Acknowledgements

As well as the published writers and industry professionals who kindly answered questions for this book, I'm indebted to those people who asked the questions that gave me a clear idea of what readers wanted to know. These questions came from writers' groups, the Romantic Novelists' Association's New Writers' Scheme, a couple of conferences and even over breakfast in the New Cavendish Club. Thank you all for your interest in my book.

Thanks also to all at Accent Press, especially Hazel for being receptive to my ideas for *Love Writing* when wine and pasta were oiling the creative wheels.

Contents

SO, WHAT'S THIS BOOK ABOUT?

What is romantic fiction? Read these phrases:

Purple passion

Bodice ripper

Pink and fluffy

Now forget them. They're nothing to do with current romantic fiction except that journalists like to invoke them from time to time.

Instead, think bright, emotional, involving, intelligent storytelling about love and desire.

Now *that's* romantic fiction!

Many people think that the terms *romance* and *romantic fiction* are interchangeable. But they're not. *Romance* is part of romantic fiction but refers to a particularly intense and close focus genre where it's not his story; it's not her story; it's *their* story. Romantic fiction encompasses everything from romances to chart-topping chick lit and romantic comedies, through gritty sagas, sweeping historicals and smouldering erotica, to liver-twisting affairs with vampires and shapeshifters. If there's a romantic relationship at the core of the story – it's romantic fiction.

Good romantic novels provide long hours of escape for roughly the cost of a single cinema ticket, transporting us through the hard – and hard up – times and never jeopardising any existing relationships. Reading romantic fiction grips you by the heart.

Writing it is like falling in love.

You can't concentrate on anything but what colour his eyes are, how she wears her hair, his naughty smile, how she'll react when she finds out about his ex, how he'll behave when the chips are down.

You shove your kids' socks in the oven and the chicken in the washing machine while you mentally arrange the births and marriages in your saga, think up a funny incident that has the potential to descend into disaster for your romantic comedy or wonder when you'll have time to research parlour manners in the nineteenth century for your historical romance. Increasingly a student of human nature, you'll goggle at your friends' relationships dissolving and reforming and slyly note the best bits on napkins at dinner parties.

You'll realise that romantic fiction is preoccupied for longer with obstacles and misunderstandings than it is with resolution and if you let your central female character (heroine) have your central male character (hero) too soon it will be a really boring – or short – story!

Book deals in the news will catch your interest; you'll dream of earning enough to leave your day job and see yourself affording a new computer and a big leather chair, having a private phone line so that your publisher and agent can always call you. (Although you might one day discover that time away from ringing phones becomes your burning goal!)

Because love sells and sex sells there are plenty of writers who earn their living writing about love: novels, short stories and serials for magazines, anthologies and websites. These are writers who have learnt their craft, studied the market and the publishing world, and who have learnt to persist.

And who, normally, have learnt to work hard.

When you're writing about romantic love, sexual love

frequently follows. Erotic fiction is an expanding area of publishing and where the boundary lies between hot romantic fiction and erotic fiction is largely a matter of opinion so, for both those reasons, and because lots of people like to read it and to write it, erotic fiction will have some pages of its own.

More on genre, later, because to know what genre or sub-genre your work falls into is imperative to editors, agents and booksellers, so it's imperative to you.

You'll need to know where in a bookshop your novel will be found and which country that bookshop is in. Your work might be published in English throughout the English-speaking world and in translation all around the rest of the world, but, generally, it will be published *from* one place. Each place (market) has its own range of popular genres and it'll help you to identify them early on. You might think it's lunacy for someone to demand, 'UK or US?' before you've even opened a new file entitled *My Romantic Novel* on your laptop but it can save you a lot of time and a gigantic amount of disappointment to know.

You'll need to get an idea of who the readers are in a particular market and what it is they want to read. It's true that satisfying an editor comes before satisfying a reader but you don't stand much chance of doing the former if you haven't got to grips with the latter.

Once you've learnt what your readers want, you need to give it to them, relentlessly, so that they stick with you for every word of every page. There's no worse indictment of a book than being put down half-read.

A good way to learn what the reader wants is to read the type of book you're going to write. Not so that you can steal ideas, characters or plots but so you can absorb and understand how that kind of book works, so that you'll never submit a book that has an unhappy ending to a romance line –

sometimes called a series: romances that are similar in length, outlook, sensuality levels etc, - or singe the sensibilities of a sweet romance editor by sending red-hot action.

Keep reading. Read this year's books. There are fashions in everything and publishing is no exception.

There are few things so discouraging as having your book rejected not because you can't write – but because you wrote the wrong book.

Try this:

Visit a bookshop and search out the books like yours. Are they in the A-Z shelves? Or on shelves containing named categories: *romance, women's fiction, historical, saga, romantic comedy, chick lit?* Does the publisher have its own section? Is your book likely to earn a prominent position in the shop? Are there banners and offers and other promotions?

Consider how your book might be placed and whether you'll be satisfied with the result.

You may not change anything but it's as well to be realistic from the start.

Now go and do it in a few more bookshops ...

HEROES AND HEROINES

It's not true to say that the only romance is a heterosexual romance but I will refer only to a hero and a heroine. It's going to drive us all demented if I keep switching to a hero and a hero or a heroine and a heroine.

I realise that it's more precise to use terms like *central female character* and *central male character* or *female protagonist* and *male protagonist* but none of those terms are fun, sexy or romantic. *When your central female character is lusting after your central male character ...* It's a bit clunky.

So, let's look at our hero and heroine.

They are the most important characters in your book. There may be more than one hero and more than one heroine. A romantic comedy or chick lit might be woven around two or even three couples and saga writers have several from each generation. These crucial characters will vary, subtly and not so subtly, from one sub-genre to another. But they'll have the fundamentals in common.

Love your hero
Dictionary definitions of the word hero include *protector*, *defender* or *guardian* and, in mythology, the offspring of a mortal and a deity.

You will love your hero.

You *must* love your hero.

If you don't find him desirable and loveable, no one will! Not your heroine and certainly not your reader. It's unlikely that you'll coax anyone into believing in an exciting geography teacher if you glaze over just typing the words.

Even if you find your hero exasperating, if you suspect him of cheating and you've given him a perpetual scowl, he must have a (possibly disguised) kind streak. Many a hero stalks into a book in his worst mood or scruffiest clothes and butts heads with the heroine but there will be clues to the decent bloke underneath. Flashes of Decent Bloke are often linked with visual clues – a crooked but appealing smile or crinkly eyes. Or a cute behind (my favourite).

No matter that his high-handedness has made your heroine blind with fury; he will haul her back when she steps out in front of a car. He might growl, 'Are you stupid or something?' as he does so but, from their first meeting, he won't want her hurt.

And remember that first impressions count. If you make him *excessively* grouchy or *welded* to his granddad's old woolly then your heroine's passion for him will be implausible even though you skilfully spin him into being a heart-stopper during the course of the story. Hero qualities should always be there if you look.

A hero should *never*:

- Be cruel to children
- Or animals
- Or to a near relative, particularly his dear old mum or his flaky sister (speaking as a flaky sister, I'm particularly hot on this one).
- Be dishonest, unless it's later proved he has been forced into an action to protect somebody else. Or unless you can make him a sexy scoundrel like Danny Ocean in *Ocean's Eleven.* – and find a suitable market.

So what *does* he need to be, to make him irresistible?

- Funny

6

- Sexy
- Intelligent
- Kind – even if it's under a crusty exterior
- Exciting
- Successful in some way

Take a broad view of the *successful* label, though. Some heroes will be racing drivers or chief executives of designer labels, billionaire playboys, artists of world renown or poets tortured by their own genius – but most of them won't. But there will be *something* they're remarkable for. It may not be their job: it might be the marathons they run for charity or being a brilliant single dad.

It will be something for the reader and the heroine to admire.

Depending upon the market you're targeting, your hero will also be some of the following:

- Fit (gorgeous)
- Fit (athletic)
- Fit (ahem! Well-endowed)
- Dangerous
- Moral
- Driven
- Strong
- Reformed
- Choosy
- Misunderstood
- Wealthy
- High-ranking
- Generous
- Damaged
- Recovering
- Self-sacrificing
- A wonderful lover

- Brooding
- Able to cope with adversity

Some writers like a visual stimulus when creating a hero. They cut out a picture from a magazine or simply plant in their mind an image of Johnny Depp or Rod Stewart. Or they create a pastiche: Rod's sharp features but the dark curly hair of the cashier in their local bank. It doesn't matter what your technique is, so long as he makes you go *phwoarr!* when you "look" at him and he's the right hero for your heroine. If your heroine is 50+ then Rod will probably be more the ticket than Johnny. Unless you want to wheel Johnny out as a toy boy?

Making your hero's age appropriate is important. This was brought home to me via my son's views on the heroes of the *Lord of the Rings* film. 'The young girls like Orlando Bloom, Mum. Only the game old chicks like Viggo Mortensen!'

I, of course, had just confessed a lust for Viggo.

Jill Mansell, author of best selling chick lit novels:
Creating heroes for my books is possibly my favourite part of the whole writing process – I bundle together all the different qualities I'd most like to find in a man in real life and wrap them up in one irresistible body! Better still, I can leave out the less desirable features that have been known to affect real men. I love it that my heroes never burp, fart or snore like tractors. (Oh, my other half has just looked over my shoulder and would like me to point out that he does none of these things and is perfect in every way. Hmm …)

So, physically, my heroes are seriously attractive but, more importantly for me, they have to have a fantastic sense of humour. A man who looks amazing but can't make me laugh would be the world's biggest let-down. Having written over twenty books now, each of my heroes has been different, but the one attribute I insist on is their ability to engage in witty

repartee. Basically, if they're not funny, forget it!
www.jillmansell.co.uk

Try this:
List fifteen words or phrases about your hero. Do it quickly, let them be the first words or phrases that come into your mind. Include his employment because that's almost always important.

Example: *sarcastic, funny, dark hair, tattoos, blue eyes, eco warrior, dog owner, vintage car driver, loyal, stubble, English, self-sufficient, garage owner, likes car races, enjoys knitting.*

Scan for any inconsistencies, like *enjoys knitting*. Decide whether it's an inconsistency or a quirk. Quirks are allowed. Quirks are good – if they're endearing rather than repulsive. It might be that an old fisherman taught him how to knit Guernseys when he ran away to sea; it's part of his mysterious past.

But if *enjoys knitting* is an inconsistency, slap that hero's hands every time he reaches for the needles.

Next, select five novels from the market you're writing for. These will be easily to hand because you'll be reading loads and loads, *won't* you? Make a list for the hero of each book. Compare each list to yours. Does your hero fit in with what these publishers are publishing? If their heroes begin by being brooding and dangerous but allow love to reform them, does yours? If their heroes are doctors or surgeons, is yours? Are their ordinary blokes really and truly ordinary or do they have some strength to distinguish them? Oops ... back to the drawing board.

Be really objective over this and, if you simply can't be, give the lists to friends, especially writing friends, and ask them to make an honest comparison.

And if you admit that your hero's all wrong – will you still love him when he's changed?

Because if your hero's wrong, your book will be. And if you don't love him, neither will we.

So, how many kinds of heroes are there?

An infinite number; at least one for every book. And what is one woman's sex-on-legs is another's politely-glazed-smile. I mean, just look at Heathcliffe from Emily Bronte's *Wuthering Heights*! What a troll! He could wuther all day without taking me to the heights but some women adore him.

The divisions are blurry – here's my take.

Alpha Male

I'm going to use this term because it seems well understood.

Although he can pop up anywhere, for some romance lines alpha male is indispensable. So who, exactly, is he?

On a website aimed at young men, an alpha male is described as being cocky, sarcastic and *busting on women*. This doesn't sound to me like the alpha male – it sounds like an obnoxious prat after five pints of beer.

In the animal kingdom, the alpha is the individual whom the others follow and defer to, possibly because he's fought his way to the top. So, think self-confidence and power; he's the leader of the pack because he's respected, not because he's loud, aggressive and violent. He's direct and he's strong – meaning strength of character rather than bulging biceps and raised veins! He's mighty in the face of adversity and he protects those he sees as his responsibility. He may think the only way to do things is the way *he* does them but at least he'll act and act decisively. You can feel reassured when he's in charge because he excels in a crisis.

He has a capacity for anger and stubbornness. What he can't do well is make mistakes. And admitting them is even harder.

He's more into integrity, loyalty and honour – although it might be in his own style.

Back again to the world of wildlife, the alpha male may be the only one who mates. So the human version must be sexually attractive to women. He doesn't have to be traditionally handsome – although he often is, in *buckets* – but there will be physical attributes ... yes, we're back to *phwoar!* He'll have a high sex-drive and, probably, a procession of beautiful women moths will flutter around his charismatic, adventurous, sometimes naughty, complicated flame.

He's successful and often there are a lot of financial rewards attached. But even if he's a river guide or a ski instructor, he's *the best* river guide or ski instructor.

For most of the book he may seem completely untameable – until the heroine proves herself the only one who can tame him. And when he finally falls in love ... he does so completely.

Of course, he may also be sarcastic and cocky. Some of them are.

Q Louise Ashdown:
How does the alpha male show his feelings?

A **Sara Craven**, author Mills & Boon Modern
The simplest way to express how an alpha male is feeling is to write part of the story from the male viewpoint, so that the reader is constantly aware of what's in the hero's head and heart as he embarks on this emotional journey he wasn't even expecting to make.

He realises that he probably has to change some of his attitudes and beliefs in order to win the girl he is beginning to love, and this in turn leads him to all kinds of self-discovery before he can be truly happy.

However, if you settle for the single viewpoint, you will

have to provide less direct clues to his state of mind.

For instance: Body language – is he relaxed or tense? Does he stride into the room or stroll? Are his arms by his sides (open), folded across his chest (aloof and guarded) or hands on hips (aggressive)?

Facial expression – is his smile cold or tender, mocking or simply teasing? What do his eyes say? What's going on behind the mask? The reader will know even if the heroine doesn't.

When he speaks can we take his words at face value, or is there a sub-text? What is his tone of voice? Does he shelter behind monosyllables? How does he address the heroine? If he's formal at first, when does this begin to break down? What endearments does he use?

What act of kindness, generosity or selflessness does he commit in order to change her perceptions of him, and make him appear warmer and more vulnerable.

And, as the song says, 'It's in his kiss'.

Beta Male / True Friend

In contrast, we have the true friend hero.

His overwhelming feature is his niceness. He's not a pushover, he has determination and grit, but you can rely on him for pretty much anything. His sincerity is beyond doubt and he'll often be characterised as a single father or otherwise pushed outside his comfort zone and left to cope manfully, an ordinary guy in extraordinary circumstances. You might think of him as Mr Right. He's got a sense of humour, too.

He's usually successful, in his own way. It may or may not bring wealth.

His *phwoar!* factor will be high and he will represent security but passion will bubble under the surface.

Q Louise Ashdown

How do you keep a beta male looking sexy and not weak?

A **Nell Dixon**, who writes romances for Little Black Dress.

For me the answer is in the balance between the hero and his heroine. Just as pairing an alpha male with a beta female can make him appear overbearing, cold, arrogant and unlikeable, pairing a beta male with an alpha female will leave him appearing weak, wimpy and passive.

A well-written beta male is confident in his own skin, he is aware of the needs of others including the heroine and it's his quiet certainty that is attractive to the heroine and the reader. The heroine knows she can't take him for granted but that she can count on him listening when it's important and supporting her through the decisions in her life.

Many beta heroes are portrayed in caring or nurturing roles: single dads, doctors, fire fighters, and gardeners. These are all roles that strike an emotional chord with the reader. None of these images can be perceived as weak and this helps to build the caring, sensitive but very masculine picture of the beta hero.

Power is often equated to sexiness and the beta hero needs to have that aura of understated power if he is to make the reader as well as the heroine fall in love with him. He doesn't need to wear it openly, unlike the alpha male, but his heroine, and the reader, know it's there.

A good example of this can be seen in the character of Jane Austen's Mr Knightly. Unlike *Pride and Prejudice* where the alpha male Mr Darcy is paired with (for her time) the alpha female, Lizzy Bennett, In *Emma*, Mr Knightly is just as masculine and strong but in a different way. His quiet, calm character is paired with the frivolous Emma. His strength contrasts with her gaiety and grounds the scenes in which he appears and, as readers, we are left in no doubt about his feelings for her even if Emma herself is sometimes rather obtuse.

www.nelldixon.com

The Loner

The idea of a loner as a hero may not hold instant appeal but if you watch Clint Eastwood films you'll find his Dirty Harry or Blondie (the "good" of *The Good, the Bad and the Ugly*) the epitome of the loner hero. A tortured soul, he doesn't forgive easily; he broods on wrongs and hides his vulnerability. When hurt, his barriers are formidable.

He doesn't prioritise sartorial elegance but if he makes an effort he can look pretty stunning.

He's dogged and cussed. Give in to love? Not easily! And if he has to rescue the heroine he'll let her know that it's a MAJOR inconvenience. But he won't leave her to the wolves; he'll scowl and growl but scramble her to safety, success before style.

I think he's a good choice if your sense of humour is tickled by pitting him against an independently minded heroine. He'll be mystified and outraged. But fascinated.

The Adventurer

This guy is really not looking for a relationship. He has elements of the loner and the alpha male but he's usually far happier than either. Devil may care; what the hell; whoo-hoo!

He's physical. He might snowboard or free fall and his occupation gives him plenty of opportunity to meet challenge head on and pound it into the dust. A marine, a cowboy or a white-water rafter, he fits women into his busy schedule when he takes a couple of days to party.

Until he meets a woman who is more fun even than his lifestyle.

The Reluctant Hero

He always has better options than to live the life he's got but, somehow, his nobility prevents him from abandoning it.

He's the uncle who's been landed with a bad-mouth festering teenager to look after while the mother's in hospital; the manager who runs the business while the owner grieves for his wife; the drinker who rescues the ugly tom cat from the side of the road on his way home from a party. Sympathy with losers, little guys and runners-up ensures he finds himself taking on faceless authority on their behalf. Rules irk him.

Throughout the book he's on his way somewhere else but he knows that if he begins the journey others will suffer and he can't live with that. Frustration sometimes gets him as far as packing his bags.

But he can't turn his back.

The Damaged Male

Although I think of the damaged male as a category, when I analyse it, the damaged bit simply qualifies one of the other categories. How he deals with whatever hurt him is influenced by what type of man he is and defines him.

There's something in his past that is making him act in a certain way. Something that isn't revealed to the reader or the heroine for quite a while, but, once it is, it sheds light on him and on his actions. If he reveals the damage to the heroine himself then it indicates the blossoming of trust.

Whatever has hurt him impacts strongly on the story and is a significant influence on his behaviour.

Which hero?

Let your imagination tailor him to your book.

For instance, the adventurer might be a:

- Dashing army officer in a sweeping historical novel

- Diamond miner in a category romance
- Feted actor in a saga
- Yachtsman in a romantic comedy

In any of these he'll be a maverick: unfettered, laughing at convention and thumbing his nose at opinion.

It's important to check out your chosen market and understand whether your hero will be welcome there.

Q Suzanne Jones
I've read that Frenchmen seem to be out of fashion as a nationality for a romantic hero. Is this true? Are there any other nationalities one should avoid?

A **Tessa Shapcott**, executive editor, Modern Romance, Harlequin Mills & Boon:
There was a time when certain nationalities were more popular than others. But in this global age we're finding our readers are becoming more and more adventurous and curious about heroes who hail from all parts of the globe – recently, Russian oligarchs became the vogue and we've also had an Indian maharajah.

What really counts, though, is that your hero is powerful and driven and charismatic and sexy – a lion amongst men, head-and-shoulders above the rest. For our readers, the fantasy of being the sole focus of desire for such a guy is the ultimate turn-on.
www.millsandboon.co.uk

Hang out with your heroine
It stands to reason that if the alpha male is a popular hero the alpha female will be a popular heroine. But, no. That doesn't seem to be the case if, by *alpha heroine*, we mean to project the attributes of alpha male on to a woman. Single-handed

dominance doesn't seem to make a woman popular or desirable.

There's one thing a heroine always is: attractive. (In fact, often, gorgeous, sexy, beautiful, fabulous and fascinating.)

More so than the hero, in many cases.

This might be because if we want to *be* our heroine then we want to see ourselves as attractive. But I always tell men it's because men are shallow and heroes have to be attracted by heroines and only stunning good looks and the body of a goddess will ensure it.

Both of these things are probably true.

A heroine will be:

- Warm
- Likeable
- Loveable
- Desirable
- Recognisable: we want to identify with her
- Strong, even if this strength is hidden for a time
- Intelligent
- Big hearted

And some of the following:

- Vulnerable
- Flawed
- In trouble
- Scarred
- Humorous
- Idiosyncratic
- Damaged
- An animal lover
- Capable of rage
- Poor
- Driven

- Self-sacrificing

Like the hero, there are some things we can't accept from her. She'll never:
- Be cruel to animals
- Or children
- Be dishonest – unless she's got a really good excuse

Ditzy but endearing

The ditzy but endearing heroine is well-intentioned and tenacious but things seem just to go wrong in her life. She does need to be endearing or someone will hang the Too Stupid to Live tag on her.

Too Stupid to Live (TSTL) heroines are much discussed on reader forums and it seems there's nothing more likely to irritate. So don't make your heroine someone that the reader wants to slap, because Too Stupid to Live means she's too stupid to love.

A ditzy heroine seems to be more successful in contemporary novels than historical. Maybe we're willing to forgive the mistakes of someone living in the fast-paced, multi-tasking reality of the twenty-first century (because, really, it's ourselves we're forgiving). Getting into scrapes allows her to battle through, endearing herself to the reader by her feistiness. A ditzy heroine lends herself to humorous situations.

Her ditziness might be the result of youth, free spirit, high spirits, bad memory, absence of the organisation gene or bad luck but if you give her an issue to overcome that contributes to her muddled life you'll ensure massive sympathy from the reader and give the hero the opportunity to misjudge her and have to apologise.

You can have a lot of fun with that.

Damsel in distress

Don't be misled, the most noteworthy thing about this heroine is her grit.

Bad breaks make her fight and struggle; she doesn't only battle for herself but may slug it out on behalf of family and friends. Wit, intelligence, charm and cunning are the weapons in her armoury. She might be manipulative when circumstances are against her because she counts it as a life skill.

Never completely beaten, she does what has to be done and doesn't search for someone else to do it for her.

Even so, she often attracts a hero who throws his weight on her side, earning her gratitude but not necessarily her trust. When he does finally get her to trust him, it's the moment on which their relationship pivots.

You get a lot of these valiant heroines in sagas, where they are the driving force for the book.

Successful and driven

She's the boss. Works hard, may not have time to play hard; she's making her way by her own efforts, very often in a man's world. This may not make her popular with men!

It may not make her that popular with women, either, if her image is as the wonder woman the rest of us failed to be. So it's essential that, right from the off, she shows the reader her humanity, her fears and desires, as well as the ferocious drive and intelligence that earned her a First from Cambridge or a successful business.

Be prepared to make her more likeable, to demonstrate that her success is not all there is. Apparent confidence might even be an act or a disguise. It's a sobering fact that these characters often mellow in the course of a book becoming less successful or realising it's not that important after all!

I'm not sure what that says about us, the readers. Don't we

like people to be too successful? Doesn't what's attractive in a man transfer well to a woman? Or do we want the women we hang out with to be warm, funny, interesting humans rather than career robots?

I notice that many of these heroines are saved from being robots by being enormously horny!

Brainy mouse

She may see herself as plain but under her laboratory smock and severe hairdo is a sexy woman. 'Why, Miss Jones – you're beautiful!' is said to her.

Quiet, perhaps shy, modest and industrious ... she's a stubborn bag of guts when the chips are down and will burst out of her mousey persona if you goad her hard enough. Try pitting her against bullying or injustice and watch her storm into action.

This character won't fulfil her heroine potential unless you introduce a hero to ruffle her. A heroine who is permanently in her shell isn't entertaining, so you need him to winkle her out. You might do this by putting them on opposing sides of a conflict.

Heroine who has a mission

She has some cause to serve. To find her lost baby, save a school, prevent cruelty to puppies. It will be her motivating force.

It will also be her undoing on occasion, making her situation worse and her struggles harder. She'll never give up and her headstrong flight towards her goal might well hurl her into the path of your hero. She and he might begin on opposing sides or her quest might cut straight across his or be a race to the same goal. If he tries to help her she'll probably reject him because she knows what she has to do and she knows she's right in doing it.

Or is she? *Can* she do it alone? That's often where the pivotal plot point lies.

Earth mother

The earth mother cares. Whether it's for her children, her siblings or a flock of chickens, she looks after things.

As well as creative and nurturing, she may be unconventional and eccentric; baking, growing and repairing her way through the book, probably in a cosy environment. Uneasy in a suit and downright unhappy in an office, she's a free spirit, tolerant and blithe.

Until somebody threatens something or someone that she nurtures, then she'll explode into action against the threat.

All kinds of possibilities if the hero is the threat!

Your heroine must have a good heart. If she doesn't have a good heart then we won't like her; if we don't like her, we won't hang out with her.

So even if your heroine is successful and driven or on a mission and you need to establish her forceful persona from page one, don't forget to give us glimpses of her inner warmth.

No doormats, thank you

You may be as sick as I am of reading the word feisty applied to heroines. It sometimes seems the only adjective at the command of reviewers and blurb writers. But it is a good one. Feisty heroines are engaging and every type of heroine should have her share of feistiness. They make us laugh, they get us on their side, they involve us in their flawed lives and, naturally, their turbulent love affairs. Exciting, fascinating, thrilling. We want them to win their fights and win their man.

The unpopular reverse of the feisty heroine is a doormat

heroine and creating one does seem to afflict many writers starting out in romantic fiction. Maybe they're trying to get sympathy for the character and they forget they need to let her backbone show.

If you have to create a doormat heroine to suit the plot (I prefer letting the characters create the plot but I am aware some do it the other way around), such as a woman who is initially kept in her place by a super-achieving husband, be sure to let her break out with an explosion of temper or a moment of madness fairly early in the book. If she really can't – maybe she's an eighteenth-century heroine and has no family and no rights or money – then make her subversive! She might ostensibly be forced to lie down to be walked over but let the reader see her spirit at work behind the scenes. Put her into situations where her true colours glow.

When another character is out of line, your heroine's reaction will illuminate her for the readers. Give her lots of opportunities to make a smart reply or get one over on someone to show she's made of the right stuff. These are moments of truth.

In real life, some women may be attracted to men who walk all over them. But it doesn't work well in fiction because readers aren't drawn to doormats.

Every heroine makes mistakes

It does seem that heroine foul-ups drive a romantic story more than hero foul-ups do.

At times your heroine will misread situations, make dodgy decisions or misconstrue other characters' words and all of these things will add conflict to the book as she creates her own obstacles.

But, in so doing, she will wring an emotional response from us and be seen to grow as a result of what she learns from her mistakes. She'll be more a heroine at the end of the novel than she is at the beginning. So maybe there's nothing to complain about.

As long as her mistakes aren't the mistakes of one who is Too Stupid to Live …

Q Suzanne Jones
Is it a bad thing to make a heroine quirky?

A **Tessa Shapcott**, executive editor Harlequin Mills & Boon:
Heroines need to appeal to all of our audience, who want to experience falling for the hero through her eyes. So there has to be empathy. A heroine who is ordinary and a little less than perfect will elicit sympathy and recognition – we can all identify with her. But a girl who climbs on her soap-box to lecture on the writer's pet cause or who lacks self-awareness and an ability to change for the better will not succeed in capturing the reader's support.
www.millsandboon.co.uk

Who's driving your story?
Your hero? Or your heroine?
If you think about this in terms of a quest, is the hero's quest more important than the heroine's? Then he's driving the story. If it's your heroine's quest that takes over then she's driving it.

You might wonder why on earth you need to recognise this but it can really help with focus because you won't let your storyline veer uncertainly from side to side if you let one character power the story. Also some romance lines stipulate which they need. For example, in a Mills & Boon romance for their Modern line (Harlequin Presents, in the US) the hero will always be the focus. For the Mills & Boon Romance line (Harlequin Romance, in the US) the reader lives the story through the heroine. I've met aspiring Mills & Boon writers who have had good books turned down because they've misunderstood this point.

And, whoever drives the story, you need to make double certain that s/he is likeable and the reader is able to identify with her / him, or you just won't get the reader involvement you're looking for.

Coupling them up

If you're writing a book which has a romantic aspect then just creating a woman and a man isn't enough. You have to choose the right woman for the right man. They have to make a good couple.

Couple is a collective noun and "the couple" has an entity of its own. It's what results from getting your hero and heroine together. You may have a friend who is attached to a man who you know is "not right for her" in exactly the same way as your hero can be "not right for" your heroine. He doesn't have to be a serial cheat but his qualities don't make her as happy as she might be, or vice versa. For instance, his lack of appreciation of the ridiculous might suppress her larkiness, bringing on an uneasy grimace from him if she jumps into a fountain and bursts into song to express her joy at a sun-drenched day. And if her T-shirt gets soaked and reveals her charms to the eight lads strolling by, who immediately take flying leaps into the water and begin a splashing match with her, the grimace is going to turn into a glower.

And the glower lead to a massive row that leaves the day in ruins.

Yet if he'd only hopped into the water as well and they'd laughed and hugged together, revelling in the bliss of a cool paddle on a hot day, the eight lads would have just cheered and kept on strolling.

24

To get the right man to fall for the right woman calls for a shared outlook more than similar backgrounds, aspirations or levels of education. Both of them need to think that it's funny to leap into a fountain and burst into song or both of them have to think it's stupid. One of each might not work. Not at the end of the book, at least – at the beginning of the book differing personalities can fuel fizzing conflicts but they'll have to find some common ground by the end.

Katie Fforde, novelist
I quite like getting heroes to fall in love with women who are not their usual type. In *Flora's Lot* I gave Flora, who's a pretty girl who likes nice shoes, stuffy Charles, whose previous fiancée lived in navy blue.

This is a good way of showing character development. The heroine can grow up a bit and become more responsible and the hero can loosen up and discover how to have fun. Quite often this sort of hero will actually be less buttoned up than the heroine thought.

In *Living Dangerously* the hero, David, was very much of that type. But there was a clue that he might have a lighter side because he wore very unconventional ties.
www.katiefforde.com

Of course, exactly how perfect a couple you create will depend on what you're writing. If it's a romance, for the hero and the heroine to end up as a perfect couple is probably exactly what the publisher is looking for. If it's chick lit then your couple can be realistically glued together with lust and love but retain their individual identities to a much greater extent.

In a paranormal romance the couple might be very odd indeed, one being human and one not. Their entire relationship might be conducted in secrecy and disguise or necessitate one leaving behind their own world to inhabit the world of the other. But they will have to find enough in common to convince your reader that they belong together.

Heroes and heroines get hot

When you're creating a hero or heroine for a hotter story, think hard what response you want to draw from your reader as well as from your other characters.

The higher the heat level; the greater is your scope to surprise. A sexually curious heroine and your reader might expect a physical, bold siren. And maybe she will be.

But perhaps she's a softly spoken librarian by day that no one would suspect of being a wild mistress by night? It could be subtler and more interesting to let her compel by intensity and inner strength rather than by striding around in boots and red satin.

A person's sex life is generally kept secret, so heroes and heroines in erotic fiction, whose secrets are exposed, have the potential to be the most complex of protagonists. They offer the writer the opportunity to make good use of their past, or their quirks, to explain whom they'll lust after, what they'll do about it, and how much their lives are influenced by their desires.

Writers of good sensual scenes understand that being sexy isn't just about looks. Presence and personality can be far more arousing.

CHARACTERS THAT CONVINCE

The good, the bad and Robin Hood

A character will automatically be categorised in the reader's mind as a "goodie" or a "baddie". You'll more often hear them referred to as sympathetic or unsympathetic characters – the first means the readers are meant to like the character; the second means they're not.

Whether we feel sympathetic or unsympathetic to a character often depends on their attitude to accountability. Do they accept responsibility for their part in whatever happens to them? Or always blame others?

Do they see themselves as victims and then whine about it?

Sympathetic characters do feel sorry for themselves sometimes but they make changes – not excuses.

Although the reader is likely to make a greater connection to sympathetic characters, we need unsympathetic characters to fling obstacles in the path of the hero and/or heroine. And the hero and/or heroine may have the opportunity to act with compassion and grace towards our "baddie". That can be attractive.

Whether you have really villainous baddies depends entirely upon what you're writing. In many relationship novels, the baddest the baddies are likely to get is to be a cheating husband or a lying best friend and conflict comes from obstacles to a relationship rather than villains. But if you're writing a saga your villains will probably be many – unscrupulous employers, cruel parents, thieves – all showing the hero or heroine in a good light. A romantic suspense novel might have bullets flying and baddies firing the guns. Paranormal romances can provide examples of evil, too.

Historical novels can reflect the bitter truths of history and it's difficult to write war stories without enemies. But this is a fertile field for demonstrating that "enemy" need not mean "monster".

Villains can be fun to create; colourful, memorable characters, possibly having pasts that gave rise to their flaws. Or maybe they're just born greedy / sadistic / domineering.

Sympathetic / unsympathetic traits can sometimes be written in a way that will lead the reader up a garden path which has a dirty great trap in it. The good-looking co-worker who has a boyish grin might eventually reveal himself as the dastard who has framed the hero as an insider trader; the heroine's best mate always ready with a babysitting service might eventually be caught sending iffy emails from the heroine's home computer. And once the revelation has been made readers will wonder how they misinterpreted the co-worker volunteering to work closely with the hero or the best friend's willingness to change nappies!

Conversely, an unsympathetic character such as a scowling landlord might eventually show a softer side of himself – probably through observing the heroine's integrity and letting it rub off on him – and do her a good turn.

Success is dependent upon clever building in of clues, of course. Out of the blue personality changes are implausible and cause your readers to make *pshaw!* noises as they hurl your book at the wall. (If you ever hear someone refer to a book as a wallbanger, by the way, this is what they mean. They're not likening it to a cocktail.)

In romantic fiction, a villain isn't likely to be a central character.

To know where you're going with each character it might help you to consider:

Which of your characters is intended to be sympathetic?

Which unsympathetic?

Will the reader feel satisfaction at a comeuppance? Or joy at a triumph?

What will the characters, either good or bad, learn?

Answering these questions will help you to write with focus.

In real life people are seldom all good or all bad; readers may well have different ideas about what constitutes a goodie or a baddie. But, in romantic or erotic fiction, we generally know which is which.

A Robin Hood character is a wonderful exception and if you can introduce one into your cast you're giving yourself the option of creating a lot of fun for your readers. Robin lives with outlaws, he acts like an outlaw, yet we never think of him as a baddie as his motives are so good.

After all, he only robs the rich to help the poor.

But ... if we examine this idea more closely we're saying that it's OK to rob people who have something to be robbed of, regardless of whether it's their fault that others have nothing. Few of us would feel this in real life – there are three cars in my family but I would be well hacked off if Robin Hood snaffled one and gave it to a neighbour who has no cars!

Nevertheless, a Robin Hood captivates us with his larky character and conviction that he's doing something wonderful even when he isn't. The trick is to pit him against a Sheriff of Nottingham, a baddie so black that Robin's flexible morals are easily forgiven. And the reader cheers every bag of gold that Robin swipes from under the sheriff's greedy nose.

A Robin Hood character can be a hero – like the one portrayed so engagingly by Michael Douglas in the film *Romancing the Stone*, for example – but is often a secondary character, so he can be an unconventional source of aid to the heroine or give the hero the chance to stand up for an old buddy. He's a terrific source of laughs in a romantic comedy, a provider of succour in a saga or a historical story. And he's bound to keep the reader guessing in a paranormal.

The key to him lies in good motive combined with flexible morals.

And even when you're creating a straightforward sympathetic character or unsympathetic character, remember the golden rule:

No one is all good or all bad.

So your sympathetic characters will have human flaws the reader can identify with and even the blackest villain probably loves his mum (and is loved by her in return. Aw, bless.)

But you really, really need some characters that the reader can care about because if the reader doesn't care what happens to the characters, s/he will not keep turning the pages – or buy your next book.

And, goodies, baddies or Robin Hood, your characters should be interesting. Try to prevent them from being stereotypical by giving them quirks and foibles, like real people. Pretty girls can understand a car engine; great hulking men can be scared of spiders.

These traits, of course, should impact upon the plot …

"People watching" is a good habit for writers to develop, to observe those around them and understand their characteristics and how they interact with others.

But don't attempt to copy a character, fully formed, from life, and drop her or him into your fiction, because it is restricting and you might have trouble staying in control of "someone that you know". And if you make them too recognisable, you might even end up in court!

However, don't shy from borrowing certain characteristics to spark off whole new characters to inhabit your mind and demand that you give them life.

Judith Lennox, novelist

Characterization and plot are absolutely intertwined. The development of the plot is dependent on the actions of the characters in the novel. If I want the plot to go in a certain direction, my characters must be the sort of people who would take it in that direction. The action and events of the novel must change my characters, and the plot must take them on a journey towards growth and self-knowledge.

So, I develop the plot and characters at the same time. Before I start writing the book, I must know my principal characters' background, upbringing and ambitions as well as the main events of the plot and the historical background. If I want to portray a particular historical event, I must consider who best to show it through. In my most recent novel, *The Heart Of The Night*, I describe the flight of the East Prussians westward as the Red Army approaches in early 1945. The events are shown through the character of Miranda, who is rootless, determined, courageous and self-centred. Miranda is a survivor, an outsider, an observer. Her experiences have a profound effect on her and influence her actions during the remainder of the book. The extraordinary and terrible flight of the East Prussians was one of my starting points for the novel, so I had to create a character who could witness and endure such times.

www.judithlennox.com

Motivation

Motivation usually proves to be the greatest decider in whether any particular character is a goodie, a baddie, Robin Hood, a goodie-who-reveals-him / herself-as-a-baddie or a baddie-who-turns-out-to-have-a-heart-of-gold.

What is it that makes them do the things that they do?

This will normally not only give you their basic characters but, in particular, will have a bearing on how they react when faced with a dilemma.

Try thinking about this situation:

Christopher asks Helena whether she has any children. Her dilemma is, if she's honest and says yes, she's worried he'll find a reason to give the job she's after to a similarly qualified candidate without family responsibilities. But if she lies she is risking him never trusting her – and she's beginning to have strong feelings for him that she'd like to pursue.

Imagine how the story could move on from here utilising this scenario:

She's determined to keep her baby's existence secret from a dodgy ex-husband.

And now this one:

She's saving up for an 18-30s holiday and so really needs a job.

You'll probably end up having two very different characters!

And you'll have two very different stories.

(Dilemmas are very useful in fiction because readers are glued to the page to find out what happens and whether the character's actions coincide with what they'd do themselves. It can strengthen that elusive connection between character and reader that does so much to keep the readers reading.)

Keeping in character

I've had students who insist that for someone to keep in character is to inhibit character development. I think they're missing the point. If Melissa is meant to love dogs then she should be shown fussing over her pooch, Bertram, or running out for dog food in a thunderstorm. To complete the picture, Bertram will lean sloppily against her legs and pant adoringly.

Throughout her life, Melissa will continue to love dogs, although the love might manifest itself in various ways and drag her into all kinds of scrapes or dilemmas. *That's* keeping in character.

Until …

A savage dog kills Bertram and, when she hurls herself desperately into the fray, fastens its teeth onto Melissa's throat. She escapes but from then on she's terrified of dogs. *That's* character development. Something *has happened* to change Melissa's character – she hasn't been devoted to Bertram for the three chapters where that characteristic is useful to the storyline and then completely forgotten the poor mutt because he's no longer convenient to the plot.

Characters should act in character and keep in character although their characters can and should develop, plausibly, in response to events.

However … to look at character development from a different angle, it may prove useful for a character to act *against* their dominant character trait if the motivation is sufficiently strong.

For example, try this exercise:
Let's suppose Melissa is deep in her newfound phobia about the canine world. But, then, a co-worker she doesn't know very well, Rochelle, breaks both legs in a parachuting accident and, as she's carted off to hospital, Rochelle shoves her house key into Melissa's hand and begs, 'Look after Guv'nor for me!' Guv'nor is her large, odd-eared, hairy hound of uncertain parentage.

Melissa discovers that there is absolutely nobody she can

palm Guv'nor off onto. And Guv'nor is *very* large. He has teeth. And he stares at her when she peeps in through Rochelle's window.

Does she force herself to look after him? Or does she go home and send an anonymous note to the police to say he's home alone?

Whichever she chooses, how does it affect her for the rest of the book?

What other choices did she have? List them.

What would have been the effect on her character, for each choice? Is it the same outcome as for the first choice? Or different?

Now do the same exercise but make Guv'nor's owner a man that Melissa has the most incredible hots for.

By now, you should have quite a selection of ways in which Melissa's character can grow in response to events. And each should offer you options in plot development because romantic fiction tends to be character-driven. You can play the *What if…?* game with characters to make them suggest great twists and turns for your plot.

Melissa, what if your boyfriend turns up with a snugly-buggly little puppy for you?

What if a new colleague is blind and brings his guide dog to work every day?

What if you're left a lot of money by your reclusive great aunt – on condition that you look after her poodle?

(And if you don't think that all of these and almost any other question you could ask her could lead to love for Melissa, you're not trying!)

Writing a biography
Many writers, including me, like to write a biography of each major character. It probably includes appearance but also

history – past relationships are particularly important – and ambitions, likes and dislikes, quirks, overriding trait, family structure, friends, car. When I've got these basics down I ask my character a few pertinent questions about attitudes towards the other gender, pets, politics, children and honesty.

Then I move on to random stuff. Where did they have their first kiss? With whom? Do they love their granny? Have they ever been ashamed, the morning after? When was the last time they had to apologise to a friend?

I always enjoy this process and think I'm jolly lucky to have a job where talking to figments of my imagination comes under the heading of "work".

One of the first things I like to know is a character's occupation. This is not only important as part of the characterisation but also the logistics. I have to say that self-employment is my favourite just because characters can be flexible when I want them to go somewhere and not say, 'But why aren't I at work at eleven on a Monday morning?' That's just annoying.

I like my hero and heroine to have interesting, off-the-wall jobs, if possible. Because it makes them seem interesting and off-the-wall, obviously. And the jobs should be appropriate, such as an earth mother designing gardens, for example.

And I find myself "collecting" crazy jobs in the hope that I can use them in a book. My latest is "Alligator Agent". Honestly! I saw a programme where this guy went around all day fishing alligators out of people's swimming pools outside their Florida homes. I mean, how cool is *that*?

As it happens, the Alligator Agent was middle-aged, homely and sort of spherical – but I don't mind giving his job to someone younger, athletic and downright breathtaking.

I'm a writer. I make things up.

I wonder how a female alligator agent would work out?

To earn a place in the cast

Every character you create must earn her or his place in your book.

Again, consider the type of book you're writing. A category romance has a strong hero and heroine who tend to hog the limelight. The supporting cast is, of necessity, small, and I notice that heroes and heroines in these novels are quite frequently separated from their families, geographically or emotionally, which prevents the reader from wondering where this girl's mum is or why her brother doesn't lend her money.

Write a saga and your cast list is likely to be much longer. Family and friends all have their impact on the lives of central characters. But a romance will only be a part of the story in a saga and so many other threads must exist to enable the action to move through generations and even across the globe.

In every book, one rule holds fast. Every character must have a purpose. If your heroine has a sister *and* a best friend then they must each have a separate function. If they both provide grubby brats for your heroine to babysit, a shoulder to cry on and a jaundiced view of love, an editor may ask you to combine them into one person.

And you may feel traitorous expunging a character from your book once she's been alive in your imagination!

The function of a secondary character is to do things that affect a central character and for the central character to react to them. Reactions tell us so much about a character. A quiet heroine might be a tiger for a shy niece but stutter uncertainly when confronted with her overbearing parent. It's up to you to explore why she's able to screw up her courage on behalf of the niece but quite unable to stand up for herself.

Essentially, you can divide your cast into:

Central or primary characters

These drive the book; their stories *are* the book. The sharpest and most vivid of your cast, their actions have the most significance and you place the greatest emphasis upon them.

They will have pasts that shape them and will impact upon the present. We will experience their emotions with them. We'll understand their quests and motivations and their attitudes to life, their values and ambitions, what they like and dislike about themselves. We'll know how they relate to those in their lives and whether they're horrible to waiters or would rescue a drowning kitten – in other words, how their actions characterise them. They'll have individual voices. We'll know them beyond their physical appearance and mannerisms. We'll know the person underneath.

Secondary characters

They take up the same kind of space in the book as they take up in the central characters' lives. Family members, best friends, worst enemies, mentors. They're developed but never so much as to distract the reader from the central characters' importance to the book. If you have a secondary character who is taking over because she is so deliciously naughty or he is so funny and quirky, I suggest you take a long look at the focus of the book and maybe think again. Should this character *be* the primary character? It's a heart-sink moment when you realise that s/he should, because it means a whole lot of rewriting!

But maybe you can keep the strong secondary character in her place if you promise to let her be a primary character in your next book? Many readers love sequels or series books and so, therefore, do many publishers.

There are a few characters that fall into their own category – they might seem like primary characters yet fade into secondary characters as the book goes on and although that sounds a bad thing it does have a function. For example, the writer might want to tease the readers by giving the heroine two men to choose between. Both characters have to seem equal contenders but, unless the writer can take the competition to the final chapter, one of them is going to have to take a back seat at some stage. And if the writer does keep up the competition right to the end s/he has to be skilful indeed to be able to write a really satisfactory ending: how can the heroine feel as intensely as she must about two men at once?

Sometimes, you'll find these almost-primary characters either reveal themselves as disguised baddies or are removed from the stage – you can kill them off or send them to the outback of Australia or something. This is a neat way of avoiding coaxing them to gravitate from being primary to secondary characters.

Walk-ons

These characters are almost part of the scenery. The taxi driver who stops for the heroine in the rain, the shop assistant who gives the hero a come-on look, the guy who bumps a treasured parcel from chilled hands on the commuter train. Don't be tempted into giving them any more words than they deserve. No life history. No ambitions. A few words of dialogue or half a sentence of description, maybe even an allusion to their mood; that's plenty.

Be ruthless to your cast. If they don't need to be on the stage, shove them off.

VIEWPOINT AND VOICE

Some people get themselves into knots over viewpoint but I think this is often because they don't know what their choices are. Let's begin with some technique-speak. Viewpoint generally falls into these categories:

First person viewpoint

This is the easy one. You tell the story as if you are the character and it's your story.

You use *I* and *me* and *you, mine, my, ours*. All other characters are seen through the eyes of the viewpoint character (also called the first person narrator) and we tend to get the narrator's opinion of them.

'Hi, Drew!' I breezed past as if I saw him every day. As if I hadn't thought about him on each of the fifteen hundred and twenty-one days since he told me about a baby with his name on it.

'Janie!' he called after me.

Giving a wave over my shoulder, I hopped onto the bus the instant it wheezed away from the stop.

'Where to, love?'

'Just the next stop, please.' I could walk back to my car when I'd given Drew time to move on. Nosing into the press of Monday traffic the bus grumbled along slowly, passengers tutting and checking their watches while I found a seat without looking round, in case Drew's blue eyes were staring in through the rain-spotted bus window.

His baby would be four, now.

Like mine.

The beauty of the first person viewpoint is that you're never tempted to slide off into other heads. It's an easy technique to master. For the connection between central character and reader, it's unsurpassed because it's so intimate, so direct and confiding. The reader has more opportunities to understand and sympathise with the central character than with any other character.

It's easier to manipulate your reader because the narrator can coax the reader into accepting his or her word for things, even when the facts are to the contrary.

The disadvantage of using the first person is that you lose flexibility. You're confined to that one character's company all the time.

Some writers get over this by having one character as a first person narrator but interpolate third person sections from the point of view of another character or characters.

But not all publishers like this for romantic fiction. They see it more the preserve of writers of crime or psychological thrillers.

Third person

This is the traditional choice for those who want to bring in several viewpoints, giving various perspectives on the action and diverse opinions of other characters. For example: Freddie is snarky to ordinary-looking girls. You want the heroine to be blissfully unaware because he's always Prince Charming to her but your reader to know his true personality. So, simply show Freddie's mean side through a viewpoint other than the heroine's, when she is not on stage to witness it.

For third person, the name of the character will be used or *he* or *she*, along with *him, her, his, hers*.

You will see references to *close / deep / limited third person*. So far as I can see, they're all names for the same technique – remaining in third person but getting as far under the skin of the viewpoint character as possible. You do this by involving their emotions and sensations. And you don't have to pepper your work with *she thought* or *he wondered* to achieve this.

'Hi, Drew!' Janie breezed past as if she saw him every day. As if she hadn't thought about him on each of the fifteen hundred and twenty-one days since he told her about a baby with his name on it.

'Janie!' he called after her.

Giving a wave over her shoulder, Janie hopped onto the bus the instant it wheezed away from the stop.

'Where to, love?'

'Just the next stop, please.' She could walk back to her car when she'd given Drew time to move on. Nosing back into the press of Monday traffic the bus grumbled along slowly, passengers tutting and checking their watches while Janie found a seat without looking round, in case Drew's blue eyes were staring in through the rain-spotted bus window.

His baby would be four, now.

Like hers.

Third person can be like a movie camera: zoom in intimately or pull out and see the bigger picture.

Do you want to write from *within* your character? Or *about* them? If you want to make third person viewpoint less deep you can leave out feelings and thoughts and concentrate on facts.

But most editors of romantic fiction want emotion, unsurprisingly.

Revolving third person moves viewpoint from one character to another. But be careful. The deeper the third person viewpoint, the less easy it is to change viewpoint mid-scene without jarring the reader from the story. This is why many editors like to see one viewpoint / one scene having a nice, clean break at the changeover, including an extra double-line space.

Their rule is: one viewpoint at a time.

So don't use the thoughts of two characters in one paragraph.

Mary Nichols, writer of historical novels
I prefer writing in the third person.

Using only the first person is, I think, more difficult. You cannot get into anyone else's head and the whole book has to be told from that single viewpoint. If you want to indicate what any of the other characters are thinking, you must do it by what they are doing and saying and the tone in which they say it. On the other hand, you can keep up the mystery and tension if the main protagonist, be it hero or heroine, does not, and cannot, know what is going on in the head of the other characters. I think it requires a great deal of discipline and careful plotting on the part of the author.

We are taught as children that it is impolite and egotistical to be continually using 'I this' and 'I that' and this is so ingrained in me that, even knowing I am writing on behalf of my hero and heroine, I would still find it inhibiting.

Using the third person gives the author a freer rein to go into how the characters interact with each other, especially the not-so-nice ones. Villains and why they have become villains are cases in point. I like my villains, but they could hardly be the teller of the story.
www.marynichols.co.uk

Omniscient
Omniscient viewpoint is also known as God-like or all-knowing. It's a third person viewpoint that allows thoughts and feelings from any character and also authorial comment –

known by its detractors as 'head hopping'. Opinions on omniscience are divided. Some find it poor craft for the reader to be given the thoughts and emotions of a man, his wife and their lodger in subsequent paragraphs or even sentences. There are others who like the omniscient viewpoint, as it allows (or excuses) almost anything, viewpoint-wise.

Omniscience doesn't exist in the life of normal people and so many find it unrealistic in fiction. One person cannot *know* what the other is thinking unless they are told. They can make deductions based on what's being said or demonstrated or already happened but they can't *know* because it's perfectly possible to say, 'I'm afraid there are no tickets left!' when meaning, 'I don't want you to come with us!' Or to smile while silently spitting feathers. Advocators of omniscient viewpoint get around this truth by allowing the reader the perceptions, knowledge and emotions of several people at once.

I'm afraid I long ago appointed myself Chief of Viewpoint Police and I hate omniscient viewpoint with passion. (Just thought you'd like a balanced view, there ...)

Happily, omniscient viewpoint is used most in literary fiction and is rarely found in popular romantic or erotic fiction.

So, am I making too much fuss about viewpoint?
No, not really. Because editors, agents and competition judges frequently state that writers who disregard the principles of narrative viewpoint put them off.

First or third person viewpoints are tried and tested techniques for romantic fiction, where stories are told in a straightforward manner without authorial intrusion, engaging the readers to characters they care about so that they can understand the characters' obstacles and conflicts and so they want them to triumph.

The more direct your connection between your reader and

43

your characters, the more easily you can build emotion.

Character voice

If you give a character a viewpoint, you need to give her or him a voice.

In a film you'll hear whether a voice is male or female, high or low, pleasant or raucous and whether there's an accent. It's different on the page but every character should still have a different voice with distinct rhythms, syntax and vocabulary according to their background, accent, level of education, age, job and personality. Individual voice will come up again in the section on dialogue but it needs to be thought of whenever you are writing from the viewpoint of one character because their thoughts will be in a very similar voice to their dialogue.

If a 21-year-old uses words such as, *wicked, minger* and *tight* in conversation, he'll use them in his thoughts. *I wrote a wicked guitar riff, today but Gus was dead tight about it, the minger.*

An 84-year-old woman will probably have quite different definitions of the same words. *I have a wicked pain in my toes! I knew these shoes were too tight.* She'll probably only know *minger* if she has great-grandchildren. She's unlikely to use it unless she's a particularly rebellious, puckish 84-year-old – which would be great fun.

Your voice

It's really frustrating to have a story rejected because the editor doesn't like your voice or says that it's not individual enough. It's perfectly clear to the editor what the book lacks but the writer doesn't always "get it".

Voice is actually pretty easy to sum up: it's the writer's personality coming through.

But I wanted the *characters'* voices to come through in the last segment, didn't I?

Yes, because authorial voice is about more than that. It's about the messages you're putting over, what you tell of a story, how you tell it and what you leave out. Your world view, the assumptions you make; your take on the human condition. It's your individuality, your opinion of how that story ought to be told.

So write from your heart and your voice will look after itself.

A writer can have more than one tone to her voice and if you find someone writing women's fiction under one name and historical fiction under another you'll possibly notice it more as a change in mood than a change of voice. The different writing names are useful for readers so that they know they're not buying a historical novel when they only really like contemporary ones and allows writers to express different sides to their personalities, too.

When my tutor's hat's on, I'm often asked how a writer should develop his or her voice. My best advice is simply to write naturally and do it as much as possible. Be yourself! Be natural. Write, write, write and your voice will emerge, as individual as you are.

EMOTION AND MOOD

Feeling emotional

Love and desire are potent. They're the rocket fuel to propel the novel, sparks and flames flying.

But show your characters feeling all the vital passions! And not just by mentioning an emotion: *Mandy was furious ...*

Let Mandy slam the door or stamp her foot or even hurl the breakfast pots around the kitchen! Let's see her flashing eyes and thinning lips, hands on hips and tossing her hair! Let her loose on your reader!

'I'm not standing for it!' Mandy's hands shook as she crashed cereal bowls into the sink. 'Your precious brother's always hitting on me and you refuse to believe it! Well, I'm not spending another evening dodging him – I'm going to start defending myself!'

She snatched up a bowl. It was cracked. She turned and hurled it into the bottom of the bin.

Pace, story, tension, character development, drama ... because Mandy showed her emotions.

OK, Mandy is *obviously and outwardly* emotional. Other characters' emotions might be more inward, betrayed only by white knuckles or snarled one-word answers. That just depends on the character you've created and the situation in which you've put them.

Your characters' emotions will engage those of your readers, so aim high. We read to fall in love, be galloped through an adventure, shocked, frightened, scandalised, titillated, thrilled, involved, involved, *involved*, glued to the page by the need to find out what happens to these characters because we *care* about them. And sharing their emotions is a big part of the reason.

Maureen Lee, writer

Looking back over my own books, a large part of each is taken up with describing emotions, how people feel about each other and every single other thing in life. I usually describe emotion in a completely over the top way. For instance, in one book when a son leaves home after a fight with his mother, the mother collapses on the stairs. 'She didn't watch him go because every step would have driven a nail in her heart. She felt tears stream down her cheeks, warm and salty when they touched her lips. She lifted her arms towards the door. "I'm crying now, son. I'm crying now."'

I feel it is absolutely essential to get inside your characters' heads when you describe their emotions, feel as they do, even if they aren't very nice. I cried when I wrote the above. I don't laugh when my characters are happy otherwise anyone watching would think I was a madwoman, but I do smile a bit.

In the book I am writing now, the heroine's husband disappears taking their small son and daughter with him. My heroine, Jessica, is naturally devastated. But a book is for readers to enjoy. I can't have her miserable for too long. There is a limit to the number of times I can describe her feelings of real despair. In order to avoid a non-stop dirge, I have good things happen. She gets a job she likes, makes friends, eventually falls in love again. She doesn't miss her children any less, but her life acquires a contented side.

www.maureenlee.co.uk

To ensure that the type of character and the emotion you want your readers to feel are in accord, it's always worth asking yourself, 'What is my audience reading this story for?' To enjoy falling in love again, through your characters? When you know what they expect you'll be able to see how to make them feel that way.

Usefully, emotions hang out in gangs. The combinations, being countless, allow the writer to create captivating nuances. Arrogance might be accompanied by fear and dislike. Hope be balanced by anxiety; joy can blossom along with relief and euphoria; sorrow can conflict with anger.

Another mental exercise:
Pick a romantic or erotic novel that you find deeply involving. Go through a couple of favourite chapters and list every emotion that your characters experience. Really think about it. Don't just pick out the obvious ones such as desire as clothes are ripped off or the fury of a screaming match.

Then analyse the nuances and learn to recognise the joy and exultation that goes with the desire. And is it misery or satisfaction that you devine behind that fury?

Note next to each one what emotions you felt in response.

Now separate which emotions you wish your characters to feel and which emotions you wish your readers to feel. They are not always the same thing.

Let's look at Joseph and Kerry:

Joseph feels
misery
the reader feels
compassion

That seems simple enough. If Joseph is a sympathetic character, a hero we wish *we* were in the arms of, we're sorry that he's miserable.

But what if Joseph is *un*sympathetic and has spent the book trying to cut out Kerry's liver?

Joseph feels
misery
the reader feels
delighted!

Joseph is vile and wicked! He's got his comeuppance. Good. Serves him right. Yeah!

Until we learn that he needs Kerry's liver to haul his teenage daughter from the brink of death. She is in desperate need of a transplant and Kerry is one of the rare people who is a match …

Joseph feels
misery
the reader feels
um … compassion again? Well, probably not unadulterated compassion because the teenage daughter's state of health isn't Kerry's fault and Kerry's nice and Joseph's not *but* … his motives are unexpectedly good. So while we don't want Kerry to lose a liver, we would like the teenage daughter to be hauled from the brink of death.

Hmm.

Everything depends upon how the writer presents the case to the reader because it's possible for reader sympathy to be manipulated. We can choose what to make the readers feel! Joseph might be pressuring Kerry intolerably, resorting to bribes, blackmail and thuggery but when we witness his grief at his daughter's bedside as he vows not to let her die, suddenly we begin to make excuses for him.

Understanding reader response is important and often neglected.

Giving reader manipulation a little thought, deciding with whom you want the reader to sympathise, when and why, can help you bind your readers to every twist and turn of your book. Which means they love it and dash out to buy the next.

Q Suzanne Jones
The last critique I received from the Romantic Novelists' Association's New Writers' Scheme for my current WIP [work in progress] stated that I needed to increase the emotional punch in some scenes. What is emotional punch? And how would I go about increasing it?

A **Tessa Shapcott**, executive editor, Harlequin Mills & Boon:
We get asked this question a lot. I think I can answer this best by describing what I want to experience when I sit down to read a great Modern Romance: larger-than-life characters who are involved in the love-affair of a lifetime, and whose emotional ups and downs will keep me on the edge of my seat until the very last page. So their romance must develop at a fast pace with intensity and sexual passion, and take me on an emotional roller-coaster ride. At the end of the novel, I hope to feel pleasantly exhausted and very satisfied!

For the writer, this means living in her characters' skins, empathising deeply with her heroine and falling in love with her hero – and pouring her heart and soul into every word. And at the end she should feel pleasantly exhausted and very satisfied also!
www.millsandboon.co.uk

Empathy

Empathy and sympathy are not interchangeable terms, although they have an element in common: understanding of someone other than oneself. For writing purposes, empathy means understanding a character and sympathy means being on their side.

Empathy's so important to the writer in terms of characterisation. How many times have you heard that phrase "get under the character's skin"? Whether it comes from a tutor, editor or agent, they're suggesting you be empathetic, concentrate on feeling what your character feels, know where they're coming from, their past, their attitudes, understand them and everything they do.

If you succeed, your reader should readily empathise with the character, too, because you've done such a good job of making the reader see what makes the character tick. This is especially useful if you'd like the reader to forgive a character for something.

Mood

What mood will I be in if I read your story?

Heartsore over the heroine's rags-to-riches battle?

Inspired by love triumphing over injury / illness / separation?

Exhilarated by a tempestuous tumble into love?

Your book may go through many moods and would probably be jolly boring if it didn't. But there should be one mood that prevails and it will help you to write in a focused way if you know what mood you want your reader to be in.

And be aware that if you make the mood too miserable for too long they might put the book down and go and do something more fun!

Tone

It took me a long time to understand tone and telling you how I came to see the light is probably a good way of passing the information on to you.

I'm keen on networking opportunities (more on this subject later) and always prepared to pitch a book to a publisher over a glass of wine and a nibble but I was once thrown by an editor at a party asking "What's the tone of your book?"

Being a bit dim, I repeated what I'd already told him. 'Um ... it's about a woman leaving everything she knows to begin a new life.'

He looked unimpressed. 'But is it deep and thought provoking? An angst-ridden delve into mid-life crises?'

'Um ...'

'Or is it a sparky, entertaining, light look at starting over?'

'Yes! The second one!' Finally, I realised that the tone affected the way that the story was told and the audience that I was trying to tell it to. And the editor needed to know how my book might fit in with what he publishes. If he was looking for a gritty soul-searcher then he simply would not be interested in a romantic comedy.

From the point of view of craft, the wrong tone can flatten a book or generate an odd hybrid, such as a tragedy full of jokey references.

All fiction has a tone created by the formality of the language, the vocabulary, grammar and syntax, outlook, imagery, just about everything about the story. And the tone needs to be even throughout.

Often, naming the genre is a shortcut to indicating the tone as you're unlikely to write a rom com or chick lit that is formal, these books being characterised as light, amusing and entertaining, couched in contemporary popular language and a conversational style.

So, if I'd answered that editor, 'It's light, contemporary, typical of chick lit, really,' he would have thought that I had some understanding of what I'd written.

Instead of thinking I was a bit of a lackwit.

SENSES ESSENTIAL IN SENSUAL SCENES

Love scenes are essential to a romantic novel, from gentle kisses to rampant sex. In your book, people fall in love, and that involves physical contact.

Although the senses don't only come into love scenes, love scenes do lend themselves to use of the senses because, through them, we experience the physical world. Employing senses will help your readers share the experiences of your characters.

We're talking about hearing, vision, taste, smell and touch.

Let's concern ourselves, for the moment, only with these five, even if your heroine has a sixth sense for trouble and your hero has extra sensory perception or an infallible sense of direction.

Hearing and vision will often head the pack – they're the most straightforward of the senses and some writers seem to use only these two. But touch is incredibly important: the satin of skin, the slithering of hair, lips on lips, rough hands / smooth hands.

And, supplying the nuances: smell and taste, which can be pleasant or unpleasant: a spicy perfume might thrill the hero as he slides his arms around the heroine – or it might revolt him, particularly if it reminds him of his least favourite teacher.

We've all read scenes where the senses are used in tick-box style. *Oh yes, her eyes are blue, her skin is satin, her hair smells of shampoo, she squeaks endearingly when aroused ... TASTE! I haven't mentioned taste! What can she taste of ...?*

Instead, concentrate on sensory effect. Maybe it's the mischief in those blue eyes that's fascinating your hero, the brush of her satin skin turning his to goosebumps, the fragrance of her hair making him want to bury his face in it.

Squeaks – no, I don't really think so. Words are good. Or even the roaring traffic beyond the window fading into the distance as hero and heroine concentrate on each other. Make it real.

Some senses can be heightened by omitting others.

Another exercise:
Your hero and heroine have come together in the dark, unspeaking. Write a love scene which has the emphasis on senses other than vision and hearing. I'll go first.

Total darkness, Grant discovered, was dank, chill, and stank of rotten potatoes. Straining his ears for a sound from the kitchen above the cellar, he imagined the man, holding a knife, waiting silently for the slightest noise that would give Grant and Jilly away.

He groped for the warmth of Jilly's hand, feeling the fear vibrating through her, jumping as a hot droplet plopped onto his arm. His heart melted to think of her crouched there, crying silently. Cautiously, the rough cellar wall grating against his shoulders, he eased her onto his lap. She curled her body up very small, her hair tickling his chin. Searching using his fingertips, he found her wet cheeks with his lips and kissed the salty tears away, as they shared body heat and waited for morning.

Morning. Down here in the clammy bowels of the house, how would they know when it was morning?

Writing classes sometimes work on the senses in a literal way, the tutor bringing in substances for the students to smell / taste / feel, pictures to look at, tapes to listen to. I agree with these tutors that there's a benefit from closing your eyes and feeling the difference between jelly and thistles or trying to describe what you remember when you smell cinnamon. Music can stir us or soothe us or evoke memories. You might even feel your writing goes better with certain sounds on the stereo, whether it's Mozart or Meatloaf. I know writers who make themselves a playlist to go with a particular book and play it while they write, to help them subsume themselves in the book's atmosphere.

When you waken your senses you waken your imagination, stir your memories, touch your emotions.

I imagine that doing an *Awaken Your Senses!* session alone at home might make you feel a bit of a twit so I'm not going to suggest you sit there writing about cinnamon. Not exactly. What I do suggest is that you begin to recognise occasions when your own senses are particularly active and work with that.

How did that whiff of aftershave in a restaurant make you feel? Was that a prickle of interest or a swallow of distaste?

You want a character to feel queasy: think of something that turns your stomach. Rancid salad cream? A roller coaster?

Writing a break-up scene? Play the song that reminds you of a long-gone break-up of your own.

If you're eating, close your eyes and really savour it. Whether it's dark chocolate, hot curry, crispy chips or plain yoghurt it will have a unique taste, smell and consistency, and it will have a specific effect on you.

Painting with the senses requires a fine brush. Don't feel that because you've written down your impressions of walking through a pine forest after rain that you're honour-bound to convey every minty breeze, glittering raindrop and ragged patch of blue sky. Less is more. A word there; a half-sentence here and your characters' senses become a shortcut to your reader's imagination.

Sometimes it's enough to write, *a strong smell in the kitchen.* The odour's probably not important or it's a precursor to some vital action – the smell of burning that sends the hero flying to rescue his dinner; the pong that makes the heroine glare accusingly at the dog. If we relate the smell to a character it doesn't really matter whether we say:

Grace gagged as the stench of curdled milk hit the back of her throat.

Or:

Working near the Aga was torture. Grace's mouth watered as tray after tray of hot, floury, fruity scones emerged in golden rows.

It's a nice smell / it's a horrid smell – doesn't matter. Engaging Grace's senses makes the reader likely to empathise.

Humans rely on vision for a lot of information – which is why heroes and heroines are generally attractive – and probably the easiest way to plant images in your reader's imagination is via colour. It works well as part of characterisation:

… his favourite baggy old sweat pants that used to be navy.

Or mood:

… pink with pleasure.

Setting:

Stone walls, golden in the setting sun …

Or even part of the action:

… mashing the brake pedal to the floor as she saw that the light was red …

Apply nuance and context. Lime green might be nerdy when applied to matching tank top and socks but pretty cool if it's the heroine's nippy new sportscar.

Eileen Ramsay, novelist
We want our readers to engage with our protagonists; we want them in there with the hero or the heroine, feeling the fear,

hearing the laughter in the voices, seeing that wonderful look of realisation when A discovers that B, warts and all, is the most wonderful woman in the world. The senses, with which we have all been gifted, are wonderful aids.

Almost every day, no matter the weather, I sit in my garden. First I sit and look: I see the way the sun shines through the tops of trees turning everything to gold; I see shadows as they advance across the lawn. I take note for as soon as I return to the house I will write down everything I have seen and I will also write how it made me feel. Next I close my eyes and I listen: a jet passes over head, birds sing in the trees, occasionally a car passes the end of the driveway – was that a shepherd whistling to his dog? I open my eyes and listen and look. I try to be aware of smells and for this sometimes I walk around the garden. I smell honeysuckle and I remember my father, dead for more than half my life, and memories come tumbling in.

Everywhere I go I do this and I utilise the other senses too. I touch and oh, too often, I taste. A warm apricot, fresh from a Tuscan tree … Sublime. Sand between my toes on any beach anywhere, warm and soft in California, wet and cold in Scotland! Don't forget the sixth sense. You know the one that makes you say, I had the oddest feeling … in that house, near the churchyard … some call it intuition.

So, you are in Paris or Wandsworth. Stand and stare, smell, touch listen, taste. No one will stare at you. Everywhere there are people who have their eyes closed, drinking in the world around them; join them and then take out your notebook and write everything down. Next year your heroine will feel the wall of heat hit her at Cairo airport – and so will your reader! www.eileenramsay.co.uk

Imagery

Let's slide a step sideways for a moment and talk about another shortcut to your reader's imagination – but, this time, from yours.

Imagery will save you from the obligation of describing things in prosaic – and possibly tedious – detail.

Use a **metaphor** to describe one thing as if it were another. *Her life's a cesspit. He's a wolf. The ship was an apartment block, towering over the quay.* An apartment block doesn't have the ability to float, we all know that, but still the reader uses the metaphor as a stepping-stone to "seeing" the kind of ship we think the writer must've meant. Broad, tall, lots of windows, maybe balconies …

Simile is characterised by the words *like* or *as*. *My insides melted like toffee on a fire. He is as slippery as a worm. She let her hair hang like a curtain.* Simile uses comparison to invoke mental images whereas metaphor suggests a substitution for a thing and might be more fanciful. Try and be original in your choices and not just regurgitate the routine stuff: *he's as bald as a coot; she's as pretty as a picture.*

Poetic phrases are like sauce – a little improves the dish, too much makes it icky.

FROM SENSUALITY TO SIZZLE
TO EROTICA

It's essential to understand what "heat level" is appropriate for your book. Are there to be any sexy bits and, if so, many or few? Will your words give a warm tingle or will they outrage your mother? (Hello, Mum! You can skip the rest of this chapter if you like ...)

Q Julie Phillips
How do you loosen your inhibitions when writing a sex scene in romance novels / short stories? I find it very embarrassing and difficult to just let the words flow out on to the page. I think my main problem is I tend to think about what my friends / family will say when they read it and I end up censoring myself!

A **Penny Jordan**, who writes Modern for Mills & Boon and sagas as Annie Groves for Harper Collins
I feel embarrassed and uncomfortable every time I write a sex scene. I always have done and I imagine I always shall do. The trick is to find coping strategies for that embarrassment. These are mine:

Worry about parents / older relatives reading the 'sex' in your writing:

Jokey way to deal with it: 'You'll find there are some pages missing, I've censored the sexy bits' – This then allows the other person to respond. During one of my library talks a reader, well into her eighties, told me she relished the sexy bits in a romance because they reminded her of 'how it had been'.

Worry about friends, etc. making fun of you – depending on how close the friendship is I normally go for: 'Just as well I have a good imagination' or if there's a touch of malice in their remarks I simply shrug and say, 'Well, we all know what good sex feels like don't we?' – that then puts the onus on them to defend their own sex lives.

Now the preparation for writing of the sex:

- Know your own boundaries, push them a little but never agree to write the kind of sex about which you are truly uncomfortable.
- Don't think about yourself when you write sex – think about your character(s).This isn't about you, it's about them, their reactions, their feelings, their responses.
- Accept that you are going to feel embarrassed – I always am – hugely so – I just joke now that, 'I'm going to have to write a sexy bit this afternoon and you know how much I hate doing them – keep away from me!'
- If someone within your close group feels a need to continually increase your feelings of discomfort about you writing 'sex' – point out to yourself that they are the ones who have the problem.
- Things that may help:

A glass of wine – I sometimes go for this option – I never seem to get to finish the glass of wine though.

If I'm really stuck I visualise something from a film or TV programme (often, for me, merely a touch or a kiss) that I found truly emotionally intense.

Be clear about the direction in which you want this sex to take your story – if need be pin up the right word in your eye line i.e. 'Sensuality' or 'Anger' or whatever it is that you want to drive this scene.

My goal when I'm writing a Harlequin Mills & Boon (which is mostly where I do write sex) is for my heroine to enjoy her sex and for my hero to grow emotionally – this is a learning curve for both of them (heroine discovers how terrific sex can be with the right man or whatever, hero realises how emotion adds a depth and intensity to sex he has never experienced before – that kind of thing).

If you are really stuck, I recommend that you read sex scenes in books similar to those you wish to write. Then type out a scene you like yourself and play with it, moving descriptions, adding to and amending them until you feel comfortable with using the language and the descriptions. This will not be a sex scene you will ever use yourself because it is the intellectual property of someone else but, just as when we were young, read books and then continued the story in our heads, so this way you can experiment and allow yourself to feel comfortable within your chosen sex genre, before moving on to create your own scenarios.

Don't pressure yourself by "expecting" to feel at ease about writing sex scenes – some writers do and are some don't. I never have but I am still able to write them.

Good luck.

www.penny-jordan.co.uk

If you're writing a mainstream romantic novel: chick lit, romantic comedy, saga or romantic suspense, for instance, you can set your own heat level, but it's likely that there will be at least an indication of sex, somewhere. Some books will halt decorously at the bedroom door, implying that love has taken the participants into a private place to do what comes naturally; others will follow the hero and heroine right into bed. (Not that I'm suggesting bedrooms are the only places for your characters to make love. Forests, kitchen tables, hot tubs …)

Mainstream women's fiction is pretty realistic. If you'd expect a real twenty-eight-year-old single woman to be having sex with her boyfriend, you'd expect your fictitious one to have exactly that relationship, either on the page or behind a discreet veil.

Q Julie Phillips:
How do you keep the passion alive throughout the book?

A **Elizabeth Bailey**, writer of historical romance for Mills and Boon
Passion is dependent on the emotional punch and this is what you're delivering in romantic fiction. It's no less true of erotic fiction, which just has a higher percentage of sexually explicit encounters.

The trick is in staying inside the hero's and the heroine's head as the attraction deepens to love. Every move, every look, every gesture has an effect. Think of those early days of a burgeoning romance: the quickening heartbeat when the phone rings; the sudden zing in the air when "he" appears; the electric flush of heat when his hand "accidentally" touches yours; the lurch at the stomach when he smiles. If you're writing from the hero's point of view as well, he will be similarly affected.

This is what builds the sensual tension and keeps it high, because your hero and heroine are still trying to conceal these effects. No wonder it bubbles over into saying the wrong thing, or snapping at each other. This passion is a held-down cauldron, easily ignited by a word or a look. Even if it breaks out in a clinch or more, until actual words of love have been exchanged, there is insecurity and doubt in both parties.

Along with the action, tell your reader what's going on inside. Punctuate your scenes with giveaway instants that show it's all seething underneath.

And if there is sex before the declaration, you've still got uncertainty.

Who's going to break first? Neither wants to commit themselves without being sure of the other.

Keep it up until the climax and save the sweet nothings for the denouement.

www.elizabethbaileybooks.com

If you're writing category romance [shortish romances, usually with a one month shelf-life] you'll probably find that a study of the writers' guidelines and output of the line you want to write for will give you clear parameters. (You are studying the market, right?) Some lines have a low sensuality level. Although it's OK to make it obvious that nights are being spent together once the relationship is fairly committed, they don't need the readers there. Chemistry is everything; explicit sex is not required.

If you see a romance line described as inspirational or sweet then there will be no sex outside marriage; in fact, no sex at all to which the reader is party. These books don't stint on the emotional intensity but they're wholesome. They're often aimed at a faith-driven audience. No drinking, no swearing and the good guys must be *extraordinarily* good.

This code cuts out an enormous number of conflicts: surprise pregnancies, affairs, deception …

But there are lines appropriate to every heat level through typically contemporary life to sensual, to sizzling, to hot, to erotic. Aiming your work precisely will increase your chances of publication. Different lines are headed by different editors and they probably won't shop your work around the other lines for you if you send in a sizzler to an inspirational line or a mildly sensual to an erotic line. Much better to give the editor in question what s/he wants.

You'll probably find that the heat level you like to read is exactly the heat level you're comfortable writing. It will seem natural to you to describe a sex scene or it will seem intrusive. You'll get completely involved in the sensual experience or you'll burn with embarrassment. You've got to write it, so it's your call.

Writing sex as a passionate blur

Many writers create their sex scenes to give the effect of a passionate blur. If it was a film the audience would see tastefully cropped minor nudity – flashes of thigh, breast and buttock, no genitalia – attractively sweating flesh, soft focus, thrown back heads, provocative movement, suggestively arranged limbs, accelerated breathing, kissing of mouths and flesh. Overt passion.

The passionate blur is considered sensual, tasteful, adult.

The emotion is excitement and the scene intimate. Intense.

On the page, the passionate blur can indicate a lot but be reasonably tame:

Easing down her diamanté straps, baring her shoulders to his mouth, he brushed a hundred scalding kisses across her throat and the swell of her breasts.

Or the heat can be higher:

Her naked breasts tingled on contact with the night air and she clung to him, forgetting to breathe as his mouth swooped. 'Brad –'

'You're beautiful,' he murmured. One arm looped securely around her waist, the other slid a burning path up her thigh and in through the slit of her dress, stroking, taking her breath away by his sureness. 'I want you!'

He entered her in one movement and it felt as if her only connection to the planet was through his hard body filling hers. But it was enough!

The sensuality or heat is quite high, here, but the words and expressions are not too graphic. But some writers prefer straight talking:

Slowly, slowly, his fingers entered, massaging inside her while his thumb settled on the nerve centre of her clitoris, making her convulse, and clutch at him.

It gets hot and certain adult words are employed but still something is left to the imagination even if, in some cases, it's not much.

Q Louise Ashdown
How do you write a love scene without losing the romance?

A **Kate Hardy**, writer of Harlequin Mills & Boon Medical
I think the answer lies partly in the question – it's a **love** scene rather than a **sex** scene, so that means your characters' emotions are involved.

What kind of emotions? That depends on the characters' backstory and conflicts, and the stage of their relationship. They might feel guilt, perhaps, if they've only just met or they're single parents or these are their first relationships after a former partner's death. Or fear that they might be making a mistake (especially if their confidence has taken a knock in the past, or they had partners who constantly put them down or blamed them for the failure of a relationship). Relief, maybe, that they've finally learned to trust and given their heart to their partner. Or sheer joy because they've finally admitted how they really feel about each other and maybe they've waited for this moment for a long time. Those are just a few of the possibilities, and it's very likely that your characters will feel more than one kind of emotion.

How do you show those emotions? Often it's through your character's thoughts (though watch out for too much introspection as it slows the pace down). How are they feeling as their partner touches them, kisses them, whispers something? How are they feeling as they touch or kiss their partner? A love scene is the place where you can really make all five senses count and make your reader feel exactly what your hero or heroine feels. And that's where the romance comes in: deep emotion, a feeling that this is where they belong and this is the person who makes their world a better place.

If you're writing in the third person, it's a good idea to stick to one point of view per scene; head-hopping, unless you're really skilled at it or do it only once in a scene, can pull the reader out of the story. So whose viewpoint do you use: the hero's or the heroine's? Use the character who's going to give you most out of the scene. Ask yourself which one stands to lose (or gain) most, or which one has the biggest journey to go on – a love scene is often a catalyst for change, both in the relationship and within the characters themselves.

And asking a few more questions before you write the scene (or when you revise it) can help you to see why the scene needs to be there and what its function is in your book. Why are they making love at this particular point in the story? If it's near the end of the book, could they have made love earlier but held off? Why? Were they interrupted, or did they stop themselves? Or if it's right at the beginning, is this really early on in their relationship and are they overwhelmed by physical passion? In which case, how do they feel afterwards and what do they learn about each other through making love? How does it change their relationship?

Take something as simple as squeezing someone's hand. If your heroine's been married to a control freak, that touch could make her remember the past and fear that her new partner is going to be out of the same mould; meanwhile, the hero thinks he's given her reassurance and support. The conflict between those feelings will definitely affect their relationship. Or maybe your hero has never been part of a family, has been in situations where he's always had to be the one doing the giving. How does he feel, being on the receiving end of unconditional love and support for the first time? How does the heroine feel, trying to break through his barriers and his pride and teaching him that he can trust?

In short: remember the emotion. Keep asking yourself how the character feels and why, make sure it shows on the page, and that will help you keep the romance in the love scene. www.katehardy.com

Erotica

Does your writing enter the realm of erotica? My concise Oxford English Dictionary defines **erotic** as: *relating to or tending to arouse sexual desire or excitement.* And **erotica** as: *erotic literature or art.*

But what is one reader's erotica is another's **pornography**: *printed or visual material intended to stimulate sexual excitement.* And you can see there's enough in common between the definitions for an argument to be made!

Often, people use the word erotica when they're approving and pornography when they're disapproving. I think that whether the writer has used the word *come* or *cum* is a big indicator! (Who *invented* that spelling? Ick!) Some say that erotica is for women and pornography is for men. I wouldn't quite agree but it is true that an awful lot of erotica is aimed at women.

What does seem to be accepted is that erotica tends to relate to sexual love, not just sex, and that to sell erotic stories you will avoid underage sex, bestiality, non-consensual sex, degradation and actual violence.

BDSM

Actual violence is not to be confused with BDSM – bondage, domination / discipline, submission and masochism.

BDSM is consensual and defining the boundaries of what is permissible with that particular partner is an element of the act. Crucially, *nobody actually gets hurt!* Anyone who has ever used a pair of fun handcuffs during sex, even those covered in pink fluff and that came from a shop in the high street, is enjoying BDSM. In BDSM erotica, sex ranges from that kind of fun role playing to dark, complex affairs full of hidden meanings and power plays.

Roger Frank Selby, writer of erotic fiction

If a scene is not turning me on, I know it needs something extra – or something cutting out. It's essential that a sex scene turns the writer on, too.

Word choice is extremely important. Raising the strength of the language has to be approached in subtle stages, as you warm up the reader. Suddenly hitting them with the hard stuff can seem crude.

Always remember that sex is basic, essential to life – a very primitive urge in all of us. It is definitely not politically correct. A sophisticated reader will often accept foreplay she might not dream of submitting to in real life. Hence the popularity of themes such as spanking …

Analysis of published material will show you that many readers feel that naughty is nice. And naughtiness comes into BDSM quite a lot.

http://myspace/interstellarvoyager

The stories often incorporate props and interesting settings – no, really, they've seen enough dungeons, be original – and clothing that incorporates lacings, leather, boning and satin. If you're stuck for ideas look at website or in one of those high street shops.

Erotica that contains elements of BDSM is popular. You only need to see the success of the short story anthologies and novels of submission and spanking published by Xcite Books, part of Accent Press, for proof of that.

Maxim Jakubowski, editor and writer: five tips for would be erotica writers
Refrain from using euphemisms when it comes to sexual parts or language. Have the courage of your convictions and don't hesitate to be explicit, albeit without vulgarity.

A sex scene does not make a story. It also requires plot, outlining how the boy meets girl / girl meets boy / or whatever gender combination situation actually came about.

Do not write in the second person. Very few writers can pull it off.

Sex is a wonderful thing, but stream of consciousness writing is not the best way to express its joy. unless you happen to be James Joyce.

Writing good erotica must evoke genuine emotions, not just sexual hydraulics.

A few more notes about erotica
You can find erotic stories online (so long as you're over 18 years of age) and *only if you wish to read stories having adult content* at sites such as www.literotica.com.

Some ebook publishers such as Ellora's cave specialise in erotica and erotic romance.

Erotica is on the shelves of high street shops from publishers such as Xcite and magazines such as Scarlet. Or you can buy them online.

Like any other fiction, erotica has to be plausible. Characters aren't rubber dolls, turning themselves into human pretzels.

Make each sex scene different to the others. Be fresh.

There are as many sub-genres as there are sexual interests: lesbian or gay readers enjoy their own erotica, as do transgender or bisexual. You'll also find followers of paranormal erotica, sci-fi or fantasy, where the genre gives even more scope to the imagination of the writer of the sex scene. Bend your imagination to the perilous matter of making love with a vampire, for instance ... You need to study the output of appropriate publishers.

And should you use a pseudonym? If you want. There's no rule but if you already write under your own name for a wholesome women's magazine or don't want to confuse readers of your western adventures or if you feel that you'll be less inhibited if nobody knows you're the writer, it might be sensible to adopt an alter ego. Just make sure that the cheque is made out in your real name.

What's hot and what's not

An erotic novel or short story is not one long sex scene and trying to achieve that is sure to give a disappointing, homogenous result. Instead, write a good story in which explicit sex plays a pivotal part and vivid, interesting characters carry the story, i.e. the story shouldn't be just what happens between the sex scenes and the erotic elements should move the story forward, not be add-ons. Erotic writing has to satisfy all the requirements that any good literature does: character, plot development, etc.

Writing good explicit sex is key. Word choice is crucial. Study erotica of the type you want to write and it's likely you'll find straightforward language combined with a few euphemisms for genitalia and sexual acts. Anatomical terms are unlikely and playground language is almost always avoided because words like "willy" are risible. The fact is that some words are sexy and some words are not! What you are trying to do is to turn your characters on in a way that your readers will enjoy.

Use words that lovers are likely to use to each other. Some will be four-lettered, some gentler. Some downright bawdy. You need to choose language that's not only suited to erotica but to your specific characters, their situation and the target publisher. That's a lot to consider and get right.

Q Janet Scrivens

Having done a few years of counsellor training, I realise how important silences are for the client, in order to soul search. Likewise, for me it is more what I don't write (or read) when it comes to sexual issues in print that's effective. So how do you make 'silences' in a manuscript?

A **Madeleine Oh**, erotic fiction writer

Interesting concept this since in movies it's often the pauses that up the suspense, but in fiction too much inaction and you'll lose the reader. It's a case of balance and pacing and that depends so much on your characters and the actual point you are in the action.

In the old days silences were often engineered by a page break and a row of asterisks. This device was often used to eliminate the love scene altogether.

In explicit love scenes it's a bit different. Modern readers don't buy erotica to get faced by a row of asterisks. The best way to portray soul searching is by internal dialogue, that gets you right into pretty deep pov and helps the reader invest in the character. But I would suggest this is best used in the lead into a sex scene or the aftermath, too much soul searching during the actual action and you'll risk slowing the pace.

Actual physical silences having no dialogue, either internal or between the characters, can be achieved by sticking to description and narrative. Again be careful of the balance here since the key to writing a convincing love scene is the precise mix of dialogue, description narrative and internal dialogue from the POV character.

Perhaps the most important thing to remember is that while fiction must be believable, it doesn't mimic life exactly.
www.madeleineoh.com

Any degree of sensuality

Let's stop categorising and return to the premise that many romantic novels contain sex. And there's a craft to writing it, whatever the heat level.

Characterisation needs a little extra thought. Both hero and heroine need to be alluring enough to make it credible that they'd want each other and their lovemaking should fit into the situation you've created for them. If you want your readers to believe that a shy, inexperienced woman would experiment with the right man and that the man would be driven crazy by the blossoming of this woman, it's up to your characters to convince. To write any kind of fiction involves the careful building of character but revealing the sexual preferences of your characters introduces a whole new set of possibilities. And pitfalls! But it's a prime area for a common interest to bring together unlikely couples or for you to spring surprises on your reader.

If, like me, you enjoy writing a biography for your characters as part of the getting-to-know-them process, and you intend to write sex for the character, you'll have to think it into his or her biography from the outset. Does he prefer women to have bare legs or wear stockings? Do men who have beards strike her as masculine or creepy? Does she truly only enjoy sex when freshly showered?

And you're going to have to make hero and heroine compatible, sexually, or your fireworks are going to be rained upon because nobody is going to believe in a love affair where the sex is a chore.

Good sex entails your heroine entrusting her body and its imperfections and vulnerabilities to your hero, and vice versa. This can build intensity in a way that less intimate interaction cannot. Imagine that your heroine has been celibate for two years after her ex-fiancé cheated on her, that you've sent the hero to break down her barriers and give her a glimpse of joy. You've put them alone together in twilit privacy and he is slowly undressing her ...

The scene is balanced on a knife-edge. If she trusts him then the potential for an absorbing, sensual scene is huge. But a badly chosen word or unfortunate confession can shatter the fragile trust and she'll wrench away, newly convinced that men are jackals. Or Jack Russells. If she's in a state of undress she'll feel so defenceless that all her emotional responses will be heightened. Drama! Impact! The writer's friends.

Diagrammatic, this-goes-here-and-that-goes-there sex won't light up the page. You need to engage emotions and passion by *demonstrating* emotion and passion, through your characters. Build up to graphic scenes using sexual tension and chemistry. And let your characters talk to each other! Let them act, react and interact. Apart from the fact that the right dialogue is sexy, it might make them seem wooden to make love in grim silence, as well as placing heavy reliance on your descriptive powers.

If you're not comfortable with explicit language, remember that many commonplace words become erotic when part of a sexy scene, words such as *enter, nibble, in, part, behind, between, off, hurry, wet, hard, wider, cry, need, thrust, deep, squeeze, free, taste, slipped, lightly, taut, tight, touch, cup, capture, hot, spread, opening, sway, up, full, angle, tangle, clench.* And that's before you get onto more suggestive words such as *throb, pulse, stab* or those easily associated with sex, such as *penetrate.*

Relying solely on your own experiences would be, to say the least, revealing. So, research your subject: read about it, even talk about it – if you are close enough to others to be able to do so. As you read and research the market, ask yourself what it is about a sexy scene that is arousing. How much is about sensation? How much imagination? Engaging the mind?

Q Valerie Bowes

I'd like to know how to write a tender love-scene without the pass-the-puke-bucket effect kicking in. I'm always so unsure of myself when it comes to showing love between my characters as it seems that everyone views it differently and what would be tender and sweet to one would be positively yuk-making to someone else.

My current heroine is a married eighteenth-century girl who became the mistress of the Duke of York and John Bowes-Lyon (Not at the same time!) She is definitely a sexy thing and I've tried to show that. What's the difference between eroticism and soft porn? I dread being eligible for a Bad Sex award!

A **Elizabeth Chadwick**, novelist

There's no one correct answer to this one but there are a few tips and guidelines.

Look at the love scenes you enjoy reading in books or that you perceive as well written. If you are anything like me, then these will run the gamut from the writers who just give a hint, to hotter more descriptive scenes. What is it you like about them? Do the same for scenes that make you cringe. Why do they make you cringe? Identify the turn on and the turn off.

Don't be shackled by thinking about the reactions and

preferences of others. Go with what makes you feel right when you write it. If you are constantly worrying about what others are going to think, then it's going to impinge on your ability to let your creativity flow. Be yourself and totally within yourself when you're writing the scene.

A love scene like any set piece needs to be crafted. Take care to get the words and the mood right. My love scenes are the ones most often rewritten.

Basically think of it as a dance and yourself as both a dancer and the choreographer. The sort of dance it is will depend on the mood of the moment in the novel. Slow waltz, sultry tango, energetic and fun twist – or dirty dancing. In fact it's a good idea to watch the dance scenes from the Dirty Dancing film to give yourself a feel for the rhythm. The bedroom dance scene in that film between Johnny and Baby is a prime example of the perfect non-cheesy, non-pornographic, erotic, love scene.

If you are writing a historical tale, then remember to go with the mindset of the period. What were the attitudes towards sex at the time? Were certain things banned or seen as risque? How would attitudes impinge on the scene? Just be aware of the mindset when doing your choreography.

Intermingle the physical with the emotional and use all the senses. That's what separates pornography from erotica – the feeling between the protagonists. Think about the power of those feelings, both the physical and the emotional. What are the sensations like? Are the sheets slippery, or crisp cotton? Is the grass cool or tickly? What can they smell / see / touch / hear / taste that enhances the moment? What will make it last in their memories?

Remember that your characters will bring their personalities as well as their bodies into the moment and that too is a vital part of the whole. Who they are, their characteristics and their life stories will affect how they react – the same as in any other

scene in the book. What are their emotions at the time? Are they bonding in love, anger, sorrow, pure and simple lust? Apply the above points about dance and sensation, blend them to who your characters are and the emotions of the moment, and you should have a love scene of which to be proud!
www.elizabethchadwick.com

And next ...?
Any sex scene in your book, whether it sizzles right at your readers or has been represented by a discreet row of dots, has a huge potential as a turning point in your book.

It might change the relationship between hero and heroine for ever.

Or even temporarily.

Q Louise Ashdown
How do you keep the sparkle alive in a book after the couple have made love?

A **Christina Jones**, novelist
Thanks for asking this question, Louise – it really made me think! In most of my novels I've managed to throw enough obstacles in the way of true love / lust to keep the hero and heroine apart until the last page – however, on the odd occasions when libido has got the better of them (and me) half-way through the book, I've taken advantage of this to up the ante in their relationship. Once they've made love, they're on a completely different level emotionally – and this is a great point in the book to hurl all sorts of disasters and misunderstandings in their new loved-up path and start the story moving in a completely different direction. For Maddy and Drew in *Going the Distance*, the post-sex obstacle came in the shape of Drew's estranged wife keen for a reconciliation. Poor Maddy,

hopelessly in love, felt hurt, ashamed, embarrassed – and her relationship with Drew was immediately back to square one but having a lot of extra conflict thrown in. And then, after Rory and Georgia had made love in *Running the Risk*, Georgia discovered that Rory, the man she loved, had been intimate with, and trusted implicitly, was involved with the rival company that could close down her own business. On both occasions, the fact that the heroines had already given themselves body, soul – not to mention – heart to the heroes gave me great scope for writing big explosive argument scenes, followed by lots of will they / won't they ever get back together scenes – and with luck had the readers hoping for the hero and heroine to be able to sort out their differences and have a happy-ever-after ending. An after-making-love-and-now-estranged relationship is like starting the falling-in-love all over again – with the extra frisson of the heroines (and the readers) knowing what they're missing …

www.christinajones.co.uk

Whenever you write a sex scene you should consider what comes next: what it changes and who it affects. What might happen when your characters are at their most vulnerable. The opportunity for things to go wrong is immense.

Bad sex

Not everything in your novel relating to sex will be good. It's easy to fall into the trap of thinking that a sex scene is going to involve glorious fireworks – but that isn't necessarily so.

A sexual encounter can be a mistake for your heroine to make before things pan out for her and the hero. Or make your hero realise that one-night-stands have lost their charm. A drunken aberration. Revenge. A set-up.

If your book has gritty elements, then sex might mean rape,

unwilling submission, incest or sexually transmitted diseases. Sexual relationships can be about power and power can be abused so if you have a nice juicy villain, you might wish to endow him with an unappetising sexual preference.

Blackmail and sex are good dramatic partners.

Sex is an effective weapon.

The sexual adventures of satellite characters can impact in a big way upon your hero or heroine – a father who impregnates his young lover, a sister who confesses to having a lover, a best friend who's being sexually harassed. A husband straying.

Sex can make babies. (If I haven't forgotten everything I learnt in O level Biology.) Pregnancy can bring a whole new set of conflicts, obstacles, desires, possibilities, joys, woes, loves, loyalties, ties and pain to your novel. Use them. They can power your book along.

ACT, REACT AND INTERACT

At some time, every writer is told, '*Show, don't tell!*'

Unfortunately, this gem doesn't always come accompanied with fuller explanation. If the distinction between showing and telling isn't clear to you, think of a play. There are actors on the stage and there's someone perched on the stage-side, speaking directly to the audience about what is happening / has happened / is about to happen. This stage-side orator is a shortcut, a way of dumping information on the audience so that they are prepared for whatever action is about to follow.

He is *telling*. His role should be brief.

In order to *show*, the characters must act. This means they'll *react* and *interact*, as well.

Different characters react differently to the same incident, to external conflicts or stimuli, to internal conflicts and to each other. Let's look at the following passage:

Josh squinting against the sunlight, wiped sweat from his face. Leanne, holding baby Henry in her arms, fidgeted on a green-painted chair outside the café. Lewis, her brother, paced around her, a self-important and probably self-appointed guardian.

Josh's heart contracted as his son's cry reached him.

'Josh!' Leanne jumped up, hope chasing anxiety across her face.

Josh wanted to run over and bury his face in soft blonde hair while cradling their son. But pride held him back.

'Hello, Leanne. I don't think we need Lewis here.'

Lewis's brow lowered. 'I'm looking after my sister.'

Cheeks flaming, Leanne passed Henry hastily to her brother. 'You don't have to look after me! Hold your nephew while I talk to Josh.'

As Lewis protested, Josh steered Leanne out of earshot.

Her blue eyes were fixed apprehensively on his face. Now that she was close enough to touch, the haughty speech he'd rehearsed all morning flew from his mind. Instead of loosing a volley of hurt feelings he found himself squeezing her hands. 'Do you think you've punished me enough? A week is a long time for you to stay away from home.'

Leanne stretched up to press her soft lips gently to his. 'Why didn't you come for me sooner?'

Josh, the viewpoint character, hears what the other characters say, sees what they do and assimilates his impressions and emotions. And he reacts. Here are some of the things he reacts to:

- The sight of his wife and baby
- The sunlight
- The heat
- His son's cry
- The look in his wife's eyes
- His brother-in-law's officiousness
- His son
- His wife's proximity
- The strain of a week's estrangement

He *interacts* with Leanne with love and respect, despite being in the middle of a marital dispute, because he's hungry to put their relationship right. The cause of their temporary separation is so unimportant that he doesn't even mention it.

In contrast, Josh finds his brother-in-law's presence irksome. His lack of interaction with Lewis is an insult.

Leanne compounds this by thrusting Lewis into the role of babysitter with sisterly lack of ceremony. Yet, look at the subtext – she allowed Lewis to accompany her to this emotional meeting, so we can assume she was prepared to look to him for moral support. Abandoning him when expedient is typical behaviour between siblings. They understand the emotional shorthand.

The motives of both Josh and Leanne are easily understood: they wish to end the marital discord.

Lewis's motive is ambiguous. *Is* he there to look after his sister? Or to make things awkward for Josh? Or is he just interfering by nature?

Another exercise you might like to try:
Put your imagination through its paces by coming up with a sinister / heart-warming / funny idea to account for Lewis's presence, something to impact on the relationship between hero and heroine.

Then list all the reactions your hero and heroine might have to it.

Remember that logic is vital in writing any interaction – *this* action will prompt *that* character do or say this or feel like that. Next time you feel your characters aren't coming alive, check that you're making them react to whatever's going on around them.

The spoken page
Eavesdrop on a real conversation (eavesdropping is in a writer's job description) and you'll hear rambling sentences, repetitions, inaccuracies, sentence fragments, interruptions, tangential remarks, trivia, lack of focus and similar people sounding alike. Because that's how real people talk.

But, on the spoken page, if your handling of the above is not spot on, then it's tiresome.

Dialogue is wonderful for breathing life into your characters, developing their personalities, allowing them to move the story forward and making them interact. *Good* dialogue, that is.

Firstly, every character needs an appropriate, individual voice. If you can "hear" your characters speak and transfer that onto the page then you're probably a natural. If not, put together a vocal identikit of your character. Gender. Age. Educational level. Social background. Race. Accent.

I've deliberately put accent last as so many writers desperately cling to their character's geographical history as the only influence on voice. *She's Scottish! So she'll say, 'Aw, lookit the wee dawgie!'* Readers easily tire of a thick accent reproduced phonetically. Produce a more natural effect by picking up the odd regional word – *wee,* is fine, or *bairn,* perhaps – and creating the correct rhythm with syntax.

Syntax is not a half-forgotten nightmare from long-ago English Language lessons. It just means the way in which words are arranged to form the sentence. Keenly observed appropriate syntax can be really useful to encourage characters to speak idiomatically (in the way natural to that person). Example: where I would say, 'Shall we go for a drink?' my Yorkshire grandfather would have said, 'Are we off for a drink?' My friend from Dublin, 'Will we go for a drink?'

Selecting the wrong syntax will make your characters seem like bad actors, especially if your book is set in period. A novel set in 1830 demands a hero and a heroine who form their sentences as men and women would then have done, remembering, too, that the daughter of an earl will speak differently to a street urchin.

Apart from period, gender and age are perhaps the strongest influences on how your character will speak. Gender influences the subjects that are important to the speaker and the others in the conversation have a bearing on this, too. A man will speak to other men about a woman he fancies in completely different terms to those he'd use if discussing her with his mother. Or her mother!

Age differences show most in vocabulary. From an 80-year-old, 'Jon's wicked!' is likely to mean: 'Jon's a bad person.' From an 18-year-old it's more likely to translate to: 'Jon's a good person!'

Giving a character a pet word or phrase helps craft an individual voice. In *Family Matters* I gave George, a young man, the pet word: 'Amazin'!' His favourite exclamation and greatest accolade. Tamzin, who fell for George, picked it up, but she sounded the final 'g', 'Amazing!' because she had been brought up to speak the Queen's English.

It was a tiny bit of characterisation that nobody but me ever noticed, I expect, but it pleased me. It was there for a reason and it helped me define the characters, as nuances can. But if I'd given every character a pet phrase, each would have sounded contrived. Less is more.

As an aside, remember that if you pick on a particular accent / idiom / pet phrase and depict it as unattractive or idiotic, you risk readers who have that accent / idiom / pet phrase hating you for ever!

Another exercise for you:
Write a scene that includes a conversation between three women. Rhianne is 20, Stella is 45 and Joan is 80. They come from the same area. Give them individual voices.

The page is your stage and the characters are your players.

Romantic fiction generally contains plentiful dialogue. Most popular fiction does. Readers are said to have been programmed by television and film to expect a story to be conveyed via dialogue. Dialogue is interesting and accessible; it carries the story and adds to character development.

What I like best about dialogue is that it allows characters to act. Put your characters into conversation and you'll find that you won't get hung up on the pluperfect tense (loads of *hads* everywhere), your story will be immediate and you'll be showing instead of telling.

But don't forget everything that goes with the dialogue: action, body language, introspection, attribution ... Without these things, you'll write ping-pong dialogue.

'How long will you be gone?'

'Six months? A year? I'll stay in contact, of course. But the corporation's success doesn't depend on any one person.'

'And where will you go?'

'For the next few months I shall swim in the sea, and think.'

'Swim with sharks?'

'Poor sharks!'

You can guess pretty much what's happening from dialogue alone but it's a dull puzzle. Without physical reactions to give us clues, we're not sure how each character feels about what the other is saying. Nobody giggles or snorts or raises an eyebrow or scowls. If you imagine the scene transferred to the TV screen, you'd be able to see how the characters react to what they hear by their expressions or, perhaps, the way they slam a door or gnaw their nails. In print we don't have these visual clues so you have to drop a few in.

'How long will you be gone?' Imogen glanced from Jack to Dieter, wide-eyed.

Jack turned his level gaze her way. He'd known that Imogen would take the news badly. She'd made it plain that she felt their partnership could be, should be, taken to a more personal level. 'Six months? A year? I'll stay in contact, of course. But the corporation's success doesn't depend on any one person.'

She paled. "And where will you go?'

Brad swung his briefcase. 'For the next few months I shall swim in *the sea, and think.'*

Dieter laughed as he zipped his laptop computer away. 'Swim with sharks?'

Imogen's eyes glittered with tears. 'Poor sharks!'

And changing what comes between the lines of dialogue can completely transform the sense of the scene.

'How long will you be gone?' Imogen glanced from Jack to Dieter, eyes shining.

Jack turned his level gaze her way. He'd known she'd love him caving in. 'Six months? A year? I'll stay in contact, of course. But the corporation's success doesn't depend on any one person.'

"And where will you go?'

Brad's fingers whitened around the handle of his briefcase. 'For the next few months I shall swim in the sea, and think.'

Dieter sniggered as he zipped his laptop computer away. 'Swim with sharks?'

Imogen snorted. 'Poor sharks!'

You might notice that I've used no attribution, also known as tagging. I could have written:

'How long will you be gone?' asked Imogen, glancing from Jack to Dieter, eyes shining.

Jack turned his level gaze her way. He'd known she'd love him caving in. 'Six months? A year?' he said. 'I'll stay in contact, of course. But the corporation's success doesn't depend on any one person.'

"And where will you go?' she asked.

Brad's fingers whitened around the handle of his briefcase, as he replied, 'For the next few months I shall swim in the sea, and think.'

As he zipped his laptop computer away, Dieter sniggered, 'Swim with sharks?'

Imogen snorted, 'Poor sharks!'

Some notable writers insist that there should be never be any attribution and that the dialogue included in a paragraph with the action or reaction of the speaker will automatically be attributed to that speaker.

I agree that tagging should be kept to the minimum, especially in the case of *asked* when it follows a question mark – you often don't need both. But I feel that some attribution gives rhythm and flow and to attribute or not is part of each writer's style. If you're bothered that you're attributing too much, go over your work and highlight all the tagging. Then go over a couple of pages from the book of one of your favourite writers and do the same. Compare.

At school, many of us had to do writing exercises where each instance of *said* was replaced with a variant: *he snorted, she trilled, he rasped, Robert grinned, Fiona hissed.* I think most of those exercises can safely be left behind with the text books. *Said* becomes pretty much invisible and the variants should be used sparingly, as they can become irritating. And you'll always find someone to point out that to speak while grinning or hissing is improbable as the lips are fixed in one shape.

Body language is much more useful to express mood. Melinda arguing furiously in the office? Have her slam desk drawers. John growing anxious about his girlfriend? Make him fidget, pacing as he phones around their friends in ever increasing panic.

Construct the dialogue to match the mood.

"Richie? Have you seen Joanne? Listen, have you seen -? Shut up and – Richie! Joanne's missing!'

Fragmented sentences are useful in the right context – to convey panic and urgency. A cascade of short sentences does the same, creating pace.

At the other end of the scale, rambling sentences full of trivia are dull.

"Hello! How are you? Lovely to see you. How long has it been? Since Kirsty went to nursery, I should think. Or was it when Ben

went? *The years just fly, don't they? Seems like yesterday and I'll bet it's eighteen years ..."*

A little of the above goes a long, long way.

Dialogue can speed pace by telling a lot of story.

"Oh, not another macho, sweaty rugby player!"

"Poor little boy. He never seems to have any friends."

"I never promised to leave my wife for you – do you seriously think I'd do that to my kids?"

In such sentences, information, emotion and even some history can be implied in very few words indeed.

Having been around a lot longer than literacy, storytelling used to be a combination of creating the story and acting it out. These two aspects don't have to become divorced just because most people can now read and write. Becoming submerged in a character is just another form of acting. Most of us can pretend we're somebody else if we want to.

Indirect speech

Indirect speech (reported speech) concerns something that has been spoken and is now being passed on in an indirect manner, i.e. paraphrased:

Kat told him that she'd been ill for ages and, for the first time, Tim noticed how much weight she'd lost. He asked whether it was serious.

Indirect speech can be useful for passing background information, especially if you need touch on the subject only briefly. But if you use indirect speech in great chunks you'll find your characters just wandering dumbly about the stage. It's a bit like watching a TV programme with the sound down.

Occasionally, I see a competition entry that is written almost all in indirect speech because the writer has chosen the first person point of view and so thinks that nobody else can have a voice. It's not true. For the purposes of dialogue it's immaterial whether the book is written first or third person.

'I've been ill for ages,' said Kat.

And, for the first time, I noticed how much weight she'd lost. Is it serious?'

Or:

'I've been ill for ages,' said Kat.

And, for the first time, Tim noticed how much weight she'd lost. 'Is it serious?'

If publishers require more and more dialogue, it follows that they want to see less and less indirect speech.

Eavesdropping

Sometimes, it can be difficult to get the voice of a character, especially at the beginning of a book, and it doesn't matter how many details of appearance, personality, history, present and future you write into their biography, you can't hear them speak.

So, what if you need to capture the up-to-date slang of an 18-year-old or the insolence of a 14-year-old or the cocky sophistication of a 27-year-old? If you need a genteel lady of 80 or a rugby-mad armchair fanatic?

Just go to where you'll find the right sort of person – and listen. Tune in. Take notes.

Cafés are good for this and it's a good excuse to eat cake.

If you are trying to avoid cake, go and sit in a shopping mall. All life is there.

'Interviewing'

The best way to garner the jargon and turns of phrase that go with a certain activity is to chat to someone who has done it; harvest from them the jargon and anecdotes.

But if you go about gathering information like a predatory paparazzo your victim might become self-conscious.

Try to get them on their own in an informal setting such as

over a drink or during a walk in the country. Just relax and chat. Be open about the fact that you're doing writerly research, so that they don't feel unexpectedly cornered. Prepare questions in advance so that you can avoid awkward pauses but be prepared to let them lead the conversation. You're the information-hungry one and they are your raw material. If you can get a discussion going then your subject probably won't dry up if you produce a pad and pen.

Occasionally, you might find it tricky to get your hands on the appropriate friendly expert. When I needed a helicopter pilot I found it difficult to find one who would talk to me. I was ignored. I was sent sarcastic emails. I got an enquiry about *the fee*. Everybody else I'd ever asked for help had seemed happy with coffee and maybe a nicely-wrapped bottle of wine so I didn't offer a fee – those guys are used to getting paid *a lot*.

So I scratched about and realised that on my list of email writing buddies was a retired 747 pilot, and I asked for his advice. He told me that my problem was that I wanted to talk about a helicopter *crash*. Not a popular subject. Happily, Capt. 747 knew someone who knew someone, and I got to visit a local airport and talk to a few people, including a ground engineer who put my helicopter prang right for me and showed me the wreck of one that had failed at take off a few weeks earlier.

You can make contacts by asking around your friends, searching on the internet, approaching professional bodies … Contrary to my experience of helicopter pilots, most people are happy to help.

WHAT'S THE PLOT?

Idea v plot

Here's my take on the vexed question of what is what and which is which:

In the *idea*, you decide your characters are going from London to Glasgow. *The plot* is the route you lay down, road by road, including the unexpected twists, blind alleys and reverses, the wrong turnings where everything seems to have gone irretrievably wrong – and how the characters get back on the right road to their final destination. *The story* is all the fascinating, emotional things that happen as the characters make their way along the route.

Where do you get your ideas?

It seems to me that whenever I do Q&A at a talk or a class, somebody always wants to know, 'Where do you get your ideas?'

Good question!

Sometimes they come from something I'm told or overhear. And if I see some stranger in the post office queue whose appearance captures my imagination, I wonder what they're like and what might happen to them.

Magazines can be a source of inspiration, especially the letters and problem pages. From features and news I get the germ of an idea to chew over, to wonder *what if …?* and *how could it happen …? What kind of person would …?*

And to utilise my absolute favourite writing building blocks:

why? (Asking yourself questions develops an idea.) *Because …* (Answering those questions develops the story logically.)

Reversing the process works, too: give yourself a fact and then play with the possibilities. *That guy can't take his eyes off the girl over here but she won't meet his gaze. Why?*

He fancies her but she doesn't fancy him. What's he going to do about it? Is he a goodie or a baddie?

He fancies her and she does fancy him. She's messing with his heart / shy / mean / playing hard to get.

They're lovers. Don't they want it known? Is one / are both of them married?

They've just broken up. Why? Who's the dumper and who's the dumpee?

The option that has the most exciting possibilities might be the idea to develop.

Try this:
Select a sensational story from a newspaper but write about a satellite character.

For example: an eminent businessman is discovered In Bed With Another Woman and, very publicly, is dumped by his wife. How does it feel to be:

The daughter of the couple, when everyone at college is reading about the whole mess in the tabloids.

The sister of the wife, who works for a tabloid!

The other woman – had he told her he was married? How does she cope with the press at her throat?

Sometimes, I'm fortunate that ideas just materialise from the cobwebby recesses of my imagination (which just goes to prove to Miss Whishart in Infants 4 that daydreaming is *not* a waste of time). I used to think that there was something wrong with me that there were people in my head who things happened to.

But, speaking to other writers, I'm not alone and, probably, it happens to you, too. We're not mad. We're inhabited.

Q Marion Fancey
What sort of content has most appeal in romantic works, i.e.. travel, suspense, drama, period drama and so on?

A **Catherine Jones**, past Chairman of the Romantic Novelist's Association
I would say that people reading romance look first and foremost for a satisfactory love story which has a great ending.

Take for example a short list for the Romantic Novel of the Year Award from any year. The list will cover quite a spread of romantic genres. Each book completely different from all the others on the list but each having, at its heart, a really good love story.

No one who read the complete list doubted that each book had earned its place on the short list but there were many opinions as to which should win. Different sub-genres and styles appeal to different people. What reaches out to each of us from the books we read is an entirely subjective matter. My advice is to write the romantic fiction that appeals to you as a reader.

Whatever you do, don't try to follow fashion. Fashions can change scarily fast so what is "in" this year may be "out" the next. As someone once wisely said "be careful that the bandwagon you're jumping on doesn't turn out to be a hearse."

However, it is sensible to try to stick to working within a recognised sub-genre of romantic fiction. An editor in a publishing house may love your book but it is the marketing team that has to work out how it's going to sell it to the major chains or supermarkets. The shelves in bookshops have categories – Crime, Romance, Historical, True Life … so a futuristic paranormal romantic suspense probably won't fit comfortably on one of those shelves. That may be sufficient grounds to reject it, no matter how good the story is. (Just remember how many publishing houses turned down Harry Potter because they didn't think they could sell a children's fantasy set in a boarding school.)

So, to answer the question, write your book and worry about the categorisation later or give it the broadest one possible e.g. historical, period, contemporary … If your publishers want to get more specific, let them.

http://katelace.co.uk

http://catherine-jones.co.uk

Whatever process or combination of processes that you use, try and scribble the ideas down. Before they evaporate. As they have a distressing tendency to do.

Getting the *right* idea

Just any old tired idea won't fuel your novel to the attention of an agent or publisher.

If you've ever had a rejection that mentioned *clichéd, hackneyed, unoriginal, nothing new, predictable,* then you'll already know this. And you're not alone! We get caught up with the love story and these wonderful characters that spring from our imaginations and occasionally forget to give them a nice fresh story.

Editors and agents see a lot of manuscripts so your idea needs a bit of wow.

This *can* lie in an unusual hero or heroine. More likely, it lies in the situation in which you place them, so don't be afraid of big ideas which have the potential to light the touch paper that explodes emotions. Make your hero and heroine the parents of babies that were swapped at birth; give her a father in prison;

have him receive death threats. Make the stakes high.

List issues that spark your emotions – abortion, neglect of the vulnerable, homelessness, dishonesty, infidelity, violence, puppy farms, whatever. Make use of your own outrage or sorrow. (But strike out the boring stuff, like politics and tax, unless you're certain you can make them entertaining, and ideas that will travel the globe, if you hope your book to.)

Make a heroine shake with rage over an issue – then put your hero on the other side of the fence. Formulate good arguments for each to ensure both feel justified in their views. What kind of person would care about this? What kind about that? *Why? How? What if …?* Hang on tight as your story turns into a box of fireworks going off in all directions.

Choose the issues to suit your book. Rape and violence are common in a saga but not in a sweet category romance. And if you're writing having a specific publisher in mind, carefully check their taboos. I've been surprised by what a global publisher has vetoed, even from a contracted writer, on the grounds of political sensitivity.

Tapping into experience
Although you shouldn't aim to make characters into thinly disguised versions of yourself, you can dredge your life for fiction material.

Susie Vereker, novelist
I was married to a diplomat so my life was about adapting to change and the discovery that, contrary to expectation, the British way is not the only way. Though I didn't plan it, these themes run in and out of my books.

Along with love and culture shock, my first novel *Pond Lane and Paris* touches on the marked contrasts between chic Paris and muddy rural England. The French / British gap provided enough material for another novel – *Paris Imperfect*. In turn, Geneva has its own sedate charm, but strange people hang around its rich inhabitants and what happens to a woman who has no money in this prosperous, secretive city? Thinking about this, I wrote *An Old-Fashioned Arrangement*. And then the heat and dust of expat life inspired my south-east Asian novels, another location full of mysterious contrasts.

A strong setting has its own character, and this affects the plot. I try to bring the interesting, different, amusing aspects of living in a foreign city alive for the reader without going into too much long descriptive detail. Best to avoid sounding like a holiday blog. The wonderful thing about the internet is that if you miss something about the setting, you can always search and find more information. But you can't Google the feel of a foreign country and that's where you, as a traveller, are at an advantage.

http://susievereker.blogspot.com

Just remember never to let the truth stand in the way of the story! If your head won't let you take the best route to drama and conflict because *it didn't happen like that*, discard the idea. What fiction needs and what autobiography needs are seldom the same.

But your experiences are yours to draw on. After all, if love has never sent you into a flat spin, how can you write about it? Or conjure up desire if you've never felt it tap dance up your spine?

A good use for a wet Sunday afternoon is to wallow in your memories. Nobody else has to see so you can just let it all rush out, the thrills, the grief, the delight, the outrage. It's an opportunity to rewrite history, too. Do you have regrets about a relationship going wrong? Write the ending you wish you'd had! Did you pick the wrong man? Explore the idea of who the right one might have been.

And why stop at your own experiences?

Be prepared to use anything that will make a good story *and* not hurt anybody else. But if a friend tells you a juicy tale that you know will make a brilliant basis for a novel, strand, chapter or scene, ask if it's OK to use it. (Or change aspects of the story beyond recognition.)

You can get some wonderful ideas from other people so try and be a good listener:

Switch on your story radar.

Suppress any impulse to burst out into an anecdote of your own.

Ask questions to encourage the speaker to expand, explore and emote.

Try to understand the motivation of everybody in the story.

Make yourself a student of human nature. There's a lot to be drawn from the lives of those around you if you don't crash around on their tender feelings.

Nicola Cornick writes historical novels:

I get my ideas from all sorts of places. My friends and family can be quite wary of inviting me round because they know some of the things they say or do may go in a book. Eavesdropping on other people's conversations is also something I'll admit to and I think a lot of authors do it! Taking my own experiences and storing them away for future reference I do almost automatically. I was once driving into Oxford and saw a streaker run across the road. It's not the most obvious incident to include in a Regency historical romance but several years later I used it as the basis of the first scene in a book. You never know when your experiences will come in useful!

Even though I write historical romance I get a lot of my

ideas from contemporary papers and magazines. I have to make sure that in taking a modern idea and adapting it to a Regency context I'm not doing anything anachronistic. But the more I research, the more I realise that there are so many themes and ideas that are fundamentally the same now as they were in the Regency period, and perhaps throughout history. I've written books which have the theme of celebrity, for example, and one about winning the national lottery. Contemporary themes have a resonance for modern readers. I also work for the National Trust in a historic house, which provides me with lots of inspiration. Stately homes, museums, costume collections, all provide snippets of information that spark lots of story ideas.

www.nicolacornick.co.uk

What's the theme?

What's your book about? I don't mean that it's about two people falling in love (although it is) but more about what they learn along the way. You can read a lot of stuff about what is theme, what is premise, what is message ... I think you just need to know what your book's *about*.

Before I begin a book, I have to know. *Uphill* is about recovery and *Family Matters* about money and family and who thinks which is most important. *Starting Over* is about ... um, starting over. Even if the hero and heroine are together on almost every page there will be a purpose to the book besides their romance – that the relationship begins as a business arrangement or for the children's sake or that there's a gulf in status between heroine and hero, for example. And your title might reflect this, especially if a publisher has input.

I'm sure that even writers who "write into the mist" (begin at the beginning and see where the story takes them) must know their theme. Or it must quickly become apparent. They need something to prevent them from rambling off aimlessly.

Plot

The plot should be the central strand to your story that everything impacts upon. There might be lesser strands winding around it (sub-plots) but that central strand is longest, strongest and ever-present. It's Jack's beanstalk and, however many ogres and giants lie in wait along its stem, it leads to the gold.

Any sub-plots, the lesser strands, should keep touching the stem, allowing characters routes from one to the other. If this isn't the case, you should ask yourself why the sub-plot is there. Maybe it's a completely separate beanstalk.

Although it's jolly to refer to the plot as a beanstalk, it's quite important, too, to be aware of the more grown-up sounding story arc (or over-arcing or over-arching storyline). It's the journey your characters travel during your book or the change that they go through. Every chapter in the book should be an episode in the story arc.

A plot is not a series of unconnected events.

Each event should be influenced by what went before and have its influence on what went after.

Seeds of conflict should be sewn to blossom later.

Conflict should move the story forward.

If you write a twist make sure it's a damned good one that won't be seen coming but seems inevitable in retrospect.

When you resolve conflicts, make characters instrumental in the resolution. Don't let it just happen or be too convenient; don't let it be something that could be sorted out during a chinwag over a cuppa. Make the resolution true to the story – don't bring on something or someone out of the blue.

When I began this book I envisaged that I would give you a list of suitable plots: *boy-gets-girl-boy-loses-girl-boy-gets-girl-back-again* or *the gorgeous ex returns* or something.

But the more I thought about that, the less I liked it. And I could envisage people emailing me to complain, 'But I've just read a book and none of your plots are in it!' And some intellectual would tell me that there are no new variations on the seven (or nine, depending upon who you believe) basic plots and all we have are new characters in new situations.

So, new characters in a new situation: that's good enough for me. Just make them do something interesting, logical, focused, etc.

Conflict, obstacles and misunderstandings
You really can't have too many.

Conflict, obstacles and misunderstandings keep the reader glued to the page, desperate to know how the heroine will solve her problems or why the hero suspects she's bamboozling him.

Let's look at this idea:

Jason meets Tanya.

They get on well together.

He asks her out.

She says yes.

They fancy the pants off one another and are a roaring success in bed.

They decide to marry or live together.

Their families like each other.

Jason and Tanya remain in love.

It may be what happened to you (lucky you!) but when did you last read a book having that plot? It's not interesting, gripping, stirring or entrancing. To grip a reader you need drama! Impact! Passion! Joy! Anger!

So how do you generate these things? Adversity. Put hero and heroine together. Rip them apart! Hurl them back together, make their relationship a runaway train and then collapse a bridge on the line.

So let's stir in that vital ingredient – trouble:

Jason meets Tanya when they are bidding for the same lucrative contract.

They knock sparks off each other.

He's exhausting himself seeing a different woman every night. She's caught up in her career and is too busy for a man, especially a womaniser.

He asks her out because he needs a date in a hurry.

She says yes because someone useful for the lucrative contract will be there. She ends up throwing soup over Jason or his ex-wife will swan in looking like a voluptuous super model. Probably both.

It reminds her why she's too busy for men. They sap her energy.

Jason and Tanya fancy the pants off one another and are a roaring success in bed. (This can happen almost any time in your novel and be a conflict or not. It's a really versatile plot point!)

Their families might like each other but, even so, are a source of pressure / disapproval or are a financial drain. Perhaps a family member needs help.

Jason's ex is in a mess and he goes away to help her out. Tanya, even while telling herself that she's too busy for men, misses him.

And misses him.

And realises that, actually, she likes him rather a lot.

And she wonders exactly how he's helping his ex and how much gratitude is involved.

So she drives her career harder than ever.

And she finds she's pregnant.

On the same day he's told he's the father of someone else's baby

She remembers she's too busy for men, especially as she has to support her baby. She moves away without telling him where.

He's enraged. They live apart, each bad tempered and sad.

He finds out the other woman's baby isn't his.

He finds out about the heroine's pregnancy.

They each have time to realise what they've lost. They begin to cool down.

Something bad happens to her and he is suddenly on her side (this situation can be reversed and be just as effective) or danger threatens and throws them together – maybe a danger to the baby?

He deals with the danger so capably – perhaps saving the baby? – that she realises, actually, a career is not the most important thing in the world. People are. Especially him and the baby.

He realises that his life has been empty until now but love is filling the void. And it's possible to love one's own child on sight.

They are in love.

They stay in love. Or not, depending upon what you're writing, because not all love stories have happy endings.

Q Suzanne Jones

I read that you shouldn't allow a character's internal conflict to stem from the fact he or she suffered a miserable childhood. Is this true? And are there any other no-no's in terms of conflict?

A **Tessa Shapcott**, executive editor, Modern Romance, Harlequin Mills & Boon:

We recognise that troubled pasts are a rich source of motivation and drama when it comes to building a character, and we acknowledge the recent popularity of memoirs based on childhood trauma.

However, writers need to use their intuition and common sense. Romances are ultimately uplifting fiction – readers of Modern Romance want to finish the story on an emotional high. So if you have a main character who is deeply scarred and trapped in a cycle of despair, you will find it much harder to achieve an unalloyed happy ending. On the other hand, a tough childhood can add roundness and depth to a personality if it is channelled thoughtfully: for example, many of our Modern heroes are self-made men who have pulled themselves out of the gutter. But they don't wallow; they have turned their experiences into a ruthless drive to succeed!
www.millsandboon.co.uk

Conflict is the mainstay of fiction and it's difficult to see how you'll write an interesting book without it – or even fill that many pages. Think drama and impact; think how to put your characters through hell's tortures and heaven's delights. And have a good, firm structure underlying the action.

The quest for a plot

A great way to drive your book and give your plot shape is to give a central character a quest. A mission. This will form the overarcing story.

The quest can be completely outside the romantic relationship. It might be to get a life back on track after a marriage meltdown. To find a lost child. To make a business successful. To restore a cottage. To get revenge. To hide from another character. To discover how a lover died. To search for someone.

But let's just suppose that the quest is for the heroine to find her dog, Slobberchops, who has been dognapped.

Instantly, we're getting somewhere with the plot because you're already asking yourself questions. Why has the dog been napped? Is his breed valuable? Has he swallowed a diamond? Has he got a special doggie skill, such as having been trained for TV? Your answers will tell you something about the dog – which can have an enormous bearing on the rest of the book.

If he's a valuable dog then he probably has a pedigree name like Lord Waggy of Pawpaw and you'll immediately wonder why your heroine owns him. If he's swallowed a diamond he's more likely to be a loveable mutt who swallows anything he can fit in his mouth. If he's trained for TV then he'll be intelligent and malleable and, once again, why does your heroine own him?

Maybe she inherited him? Or was given him as a puppy by a breeder in gratitude for saving the life of the breeder's son? Maybe she's a dog trainer by profession? If he's the loveable mutt, perhaps she saved him from the rescue centre and he ate the diamond because the diamond smugglers were dopy enough to hide it in a sandwich.

Now you need to decide on the hero's role. Maybe he's a policeman on the trail of the dognappers? Or a dognapper? A journalist reporting on a spate of dognappings? From the canine insurance company out to check the dognapping isn't an insurance scam? Maybe he says Slobberchops is *his* dog! The option you choose will tell you something about your hero's character, particularly if you choose for the hero to be a dognapper and Slobberchops to be the mutt who ate the diamond. Does that mean that your hero is a diamond smuggler, too? Are you certain that you're going to be able to make him attractive and sympathetic enough for the heroine to fall in love with a crook …?

OK, I've just thought about George Clooney as Danny Ocean

again – yup. That works.

It will weaken the plot if you don't give the hero his own agenda. If he just bumps into the heroine one day and decides to spend the next thirty chapters helping her find her dog, both he and the plot are going to be wishy-washy. And where is your conflict? Of course, you could have him *pretend* to be on the quest only to help the heroine – and then have him reveal his real agenda later.

Were I working on this plot for a novel I would, by now, have dragged out my A3 pad. It's a cheapo thing, sold from a pound shop as a child's sketchbook. I like it for its size, especially if I open it at a double-page, providing loads of room to create what used to be called, at one of my schools, a spider plan. It's now known as a mind map, which sounds cooler.

I write the heroine's quest in the middle and my first set of questions (about why the dog has been napped) encircling that. Taking one question at a time I'd explore its possibilities, letting my thoughts radiate outwards.

The value of the mind map technique is that all ideas are, initially, given equal prominence but those that are less exciting peter out naturally. The idea that takes over the page as I ask myself, *why? What if …? How? When?* is the one I work on.

Because the possibilities are jotted down haphazardly my mind is open to the best, most dramatic or unexpected route to take, trying the plot out this way and that way. If I plot in one direction, like a flow chart, I feel that's the only possible journey for my characters. And that's bad.

Some authors write notes on cards, one point per card, then try them running in various orders. It's like taking a dress into the changing room in two sizes, two colours, with three jackets, four pairs of shoes and five hats. You try various combinations until you find the one you like.

Loosely speaking, I've never varied from the beginning /

middle / end structure taught at primary school. I concentrate on conflict / turning point / resolution and I certainly don't think that the beginning, middle and end should be of equal proportions, but I do feel they should all be in there, split into episodes (chapters).

Each chapter should fulfil at least two purposes, such as to progress a relationship, show a side of a character, unfold a sub-plot or allow a villain to reveal himself. And always, always, they form a step towards the climax to the story.

Working up to it

I need a lot of info before I begin a novel. I write about the characters – you could call this a bio, I suppose, although it's more of a compost heap of information / history / thoughts – I like to look at major characters from various points of view. What does the hero think of the heroine? How does this compare with how her dad views her? Or her best friend? Or her (ex)husband / boyfriend? The contrast between how the hero sees the heroine and how another significant other views her is frequently crucial.

There are also certain details that I feel I simply have to know. I like cars, so like to discover which car and character belong together. A car reflects financial status, regard for material things or the environment, favourite colours, how cool the character is, or eccentric, if they enjoy the sensation of speed, are timid, make provision for children or pets. An off-the-wall heroine might drive a mini painted all over by toadstools. A military enthusiast may have a deep love for his restored jeep.

Getting to know the characters is a personal process and it doesn't matter how you do it because, like an iceberg, 90% of these biographies don't show in the end. They're under the surface.

Jan Jones writes Regency romance, contemporary romantic comedy and short stories for women's magazines.

If you're writing historical romance, I think you have to be in love with the period in which your books are set. It's no good picking an era and thinking you'll grab a few facts from the internet to colour in the background – your readers will know they are being short-changed. I've always been fascinated by the Regency era, so it is never a hardship to spend time looking at the fashions of the day, studying contemporary newspapers to get a feel for what was going on, reading books that were published then, going to revivals of Georgian and Regency plays.

The internet is a wonderful tool in which I can lose myself for days, but I also find visiting actual places invaluable. For my Newmarket Regencies I only have to go a few miles to walk down the very streets that my hero and heroine travel. The houses and shops they would see are still there, in amongst more modern buildings. At home I have old maps and local history books and the library is rich in local resources. I'm particularly lucky in that Newmarket houses the National Horseracing Museum, useful for *Fortunate Wager*, which is set in a Regency racing stable!

And then, once I've steeped myself in the culture, surrounded myself with the sights and smells and feel of the setting, got right into my characters' mindsets, the actual writing of the book can flow relatively unhindered because I don't have to worry about the externals any more. I know where I am in time and space.

And plotting the novels themselves? At the start of every book, I've got my people, I've got the opening dilemma, I know roughly how it's going to end and a couple of stops along the way. The rest is up to them.

www.jan-jones.co.uk

Beginning it

I have to know the novel's jumping off point and roughly where it's going – sometimes very roughly indeed! It might only be that the heroine might eventually decide that even if she ends up with such-and-such, she won't be reliant on him for fulfilment. Then comes a brewing period when ideas come and these, too, I jot down.

When my compost heap includes mind map, biographies and general jottings and I know the end of the book, that's when I'm ready to type in: *Chapter 1*.

I used to "write into the mist" once I had some idea of character. It was fun but I don't think it's a coincidence that *Uphill all the Way* was the first book I planned and the first to get a publisher. I write in a focused way if I have an end in sight.

To plan, or not to plan, is personal. There are no rules. I know bestselling authors who say they just let the characters do the plotting. They must be more instinctive in their storytelling than I am.

Whatever your technique, you should write in a focused way, not like one of those stand up comics who tell you a story but keep rambling off the subject so that they take half-an-hour to tell a five-minute joke.

Another exercise:

Whatever your normal plotting technique, try something else.

If you're a planner, begin a story with just a couple of characters to guide you. If you like to write into the mist, make a proper plan. Write first thing in the morning or last thing at night; write out five themes on cards then pick one, eyes closed; take the first page of a novel and make each sentence the first line of a chapter.

Just hop out of your groove and try something different. If you don't like the result you need never do it again – but you never know when something's really going to suit you.

Title

How important is a title?

VERY!

Unless you're a bestselling writer who has a crowd of readers on the edge of their seats for your next book regardless of what it's called, the title is the first opportunity you and your publisher have to grab the attention of a reader.

The title drags the reader into the story. Functional, whimsical, intriguing; it can enhance the theme and give the reader satisfaction when its meaning becomes clear.

Top of your list, though: it should be appealing. I've also had a tip from a fiction buyer that the best thing a title can be is *memorable*. That's why so many titles are common phrases or reminiscent of a famous song or poem.

Its primary purpose is to sell the book.

Writing tutorials might arm you with various techniques to conjure up the perfect title but I think you need to apply common sense. If you see an extravagant claim that the only title that will sell contains one verb and one noun, and that's it, nothing else, look at the bestseller list and see if that's true. Is it? Nope.

Writing a title is a black art but gimmicks aren't going to serve you as well as a combination of common sense and inspiration.

Lyn Vernham, Director, Choc Lit

A title communicates your book's contents at each stage of the route to market: to agents, publishers, booksellers and, last but not least, readers. So it's worth giving it plenty of thought up front and – even though the publisher has the final say – asking to be kept involved.

For the competitive world of mainstream romantic fiction, make your title punchy, interesting and easy to remember. Avoid words that are hard to spell or pronounce, or that may have negative connotations. Finally, check how your title comes across without any supporting material, such as the book jacket.

The internet and how titles work electronically must also be considered. Where would your title appear on search engines, and how easy would it be to find? Could you register it as a domain name? If a book having a similar title has already been published, does it detract from yours or can you turn it to your advantage? These are all important factors in marketing and selling books today.

www.choc-lit.co.uk

Another exercise to try:

If the perfect title hasn't come to you yet, write a few paragraphs entitled: *What My Book is About*. Write it as if you're telling a friend who you know will think you're incredibly clever to have written a book and will want to hear all about it, so that you don't feel apologetic, self-conscious or suffer from that awful moment that all writers know – when they become convinced that every word deserves to be flushed down the toilet.

That's never true.

Don't agonise over these paragraphs – dash them off. Now look over what you've written. Highlight any words that you feel are key, any phrases that strike you as neat / quirky / evocative / appealing / lively / impressive. And soon you'll find you have a list to work with, to play around with, to swap with each other and analyse for reader appeal.

Study books that are recently published and might be found

in the same section as yours. What kinds of titles are popular? One word? Whole sentences? *Something and something? Someone of Somewhere?* Phrases? Proverbs? Popular sayings or lines of songs that have been twisted to suit the book? Jokes? Puns? Are they dramatic? Cutesy? Enigmatic? Thematic? Smutty? Intriguing? Related to location? Deliberately ungrammatical or misspelt? Emotional? Suggestive? Referring to popular culture – i.e. a twist on the title of a megahit reality TV show?

It probably doesn't need to be said but keep in mind what kind of book you're writing. *Lack! My Lord's Lost Love!* isn't going to make it as a contemporary romance. *Chix R Us* will bomb as a historical.

But the truth is that you can spend a month searching for *the* perfect title, only for your publisher to change it.

This is true of some romance lines but any publisher will change the title if they don't think it's appealing enough. It's their job to market and sell the book so they see title as their domain. Which is not unreasonable. And their title may be better (more marketable) than yours.

This is a good time to write yourself a note: *The editor may not always be right but s/he is always the editor.* Because title changes may be the first experience you have of your book no longer being yours alone, once you begin selling rights to it. They're called rights for a reason.

On the other side of the coin, contracts have been awarded to fantastic titles without the book being read! In fact, an editor once told me that she was engaged in an auction for one. Which means that the writer of that book had, effectively, written the other 80,000 words for nothing.

Prologue
Many books don't need one.

But, in case yours does – what *is* a prologue? Typically, it's three to five pages of introductory material. Its importance often doesn't become clear until it's revealed to be a catalyst or significant background story. It's often set at a different time to the rest of the novel.

Are prologues necessary? Take out the prologue and if the entire plot still makes perfect sense, chances are the prologue was written to set the mood. But if it introduces a crucial scene that will impact the main plot, it's earning its place.

That said, I've noticed some prologues seem to be merely interesting – integral to the book but could slot in elsewhere. They provide an extra hook and maybe a bonus to the reader by taking the form of a letter or a dream, fitting into the prologue model of being short and self-contained and perhaps introducing a significant character. It can be an opportunity to write something which has an experimental tone.

While reading a prologue, the readers know full well that the real story is waiting because the first chapter still has to be the first chapter, and it takes extra mental energy to immerse oneself in a world from two angles.

You're asking more of them. Make sure it's worth it.

Chapter 1

You've probably heard the saying that the first page sells the book (and the last page sells the next one).

Publishers like the first page of a romantic novel to grab the reader and haul them into a first chapter that sweeps the reader along until nothing else will do but to read the rest of the book. They want reviewers to shout:

'It's a page-turner!'

'Unputdownable!'

They want to turn browsers into buyers; a common thing for a browser to do is to just read page one so some writers go for an explosive or shocking first sentence specifically to capture this kind of buyer. They're making an offer to the reader: *Read on and I'll tell you what's behind this startling first line.*

Make page one appetising. Riveting, hooky, intriguing; make it drag the reader into page two.

If your plot centres around a quest, introduce it.

But most of all, introduce your reader to the central character and make them connect. Make the character resonate; make the reader care what happens to her or him. Make the first page the first step in the character's journey through the book.

Another exercise:

Write down, in a couple of sentences, an intriguing action. Maybe your heroine or hero is careering downhill on rollerskates. Climbing out of a window. Running. Grabbing someone from behind. Sheltering a child in her arms.

Now make sure that the action:

- Gives the impression that the heroine or hero is at a point where everything is changing
- Poses a question that the reader will discover the answer to by reading on
- Makes them itch to do so

It might be a love scene, a conflict, a humiliation, sad, joyous, frightening; but it will set the tone for the book, on-theme and on-topic. There's not much point writing a great first chapter if the rest of the book turns out to be about something else.

If you list your novel's conflicts, you might be able to sew the seeds now. Make your hero turn away from the sight of a funeral in Chapter 1 if you want to let it unfurl later that he has just laid his best friend to rest.

Your first chapter should involve one or more of the protagonists – meeting them first will tell the reader who is important in the book. Some romance lines will want hero and heroine to meet in Chapter 1.

Consider having two hooks in the first pages:

The action / incident / conflict / confrontational one.

The insightful one; where the reader will feel that the character has awarded the reader a glimpse into his or her heart.

What to leave out of Chapter 1

If you think of Chapter 1 as an entrance corridor to the rest of the book, you'll see that it needs to be uncluttered so that the reader can move forward through it.

You'll clutter the corridor up if you include:

Too much scene-setting

Backstory

Flashbacks

All of the above are static and you want Chapter 1 to have impetus. *You* need to know the backstory so it's easy to assume that the reader does, too, but Chapter 1 should be teasing them with information, not dumping it on them. So, while: *Victoria pulled away from Nick. He didn't seem to get what "ex" as in "ex-husband" actually meant,* might provide a heavy hint about the history between Victoria and Nick, the first chapter is not the place to flash back to the whole story of their divorce, her affair or his lies.

And if you give away too much of the story to begin with, your readers will be bored in ten pages and never enjoy the anticipation of embarking on an adventure with the characters.

Neither should you be like a bad host at a party and introduce them to every character in one breath. Chances are that the reader will engage with none of them.

Chapter 2

I'm not going to go through a whole book chapter by chapter but it's worth mentioning that although Chapter 2 (and beyond) is far more flexible than the Prologue and Chapter 1, it can have certain characteristics:

It can almost be another Chapter 1, just as hooky and demanding, introducing a whole new character and/or situation.

It can be a continuance of or reaction to the dramatic situation contained in Chapter 1.

Or the background stuff you need to rationalise what has just taken the reader's breath away in Chapter 1. Yup! You can have a flashback now. If you're certain that you need one and it wouldn't be better to bring the same information out in conversation / confrontation / introspection.

Or a place for readers to catch their breath by a complete change of pace.

All chapters

Try making every chapter open at a point of significance, exactly like a short story – bounce into the action or have somebody say something hookily surprising or intriguing.

Slam out of chapters using drama, emotion, twists and surprises. The final page of the chapter is a good place for people to end a reading session – at least that's what the reader thinks! I think it's a good place to try and stop them. If they're reading in bed it doesn't matter if they're shattered and they have to get up in the morning. Don't let them put out that light. Make them unable to resist turning the page.

One way to do this is to pose a question on the last page of the chapter and answer it on the first page of the next.

Last page of the chapter: Henrietta has paid for her lunch and is walking across the cafeteria with her laden tray. Mae reaches out a foot …

In an instant, Henrietta's lunch is spread across the lino and Henrietta herself is sprawled on top of it. Her knickers are showing, her top is glooped with tomato soup and her new sandals have a broken heel. *How will Henrietta react?*

Cry?

Rub Mae's nose in the mess? (Tempting.)

Announce that she's just been given the job as Mae's new boss? (This is my favourite: play the long game and make Mae suffer.)

But don't tell the readers yet!

Maybe let Henrietta lift her head and fix Mae with a stare. Poise her on the brink of reaction and let her teeter there.

First page of the next chapter: now you give the answer.

Fight the flab, tighten the sag, keep the tension

Having written a roller-coaster of a first chapter and glued your reader to Chapter 2, you don't want to find that the rest of the book doesn't live up to your excellent beginning. We've all read books like that. It's as if the writer thinks that because s/he's begun her marriage to the reader happily, s/he can now stop watching her waistline.

Don't let your reader start flirting with other books. Make sure you have no padding, no trivia, no waffling, dead ends (unless they're by design and will suddenly be seen to have purpose), trailing threads (unless you're writing a series and the thread will reappear in a different book), indulgent descriptions or dead weight to disenchant the reader.

In your second draft, if not your first, send your book to fat camp. Don't let it carry any excess. It's bad for its heart.

Sag can be more difficult to deal with because you might not be able to see where the problem lies. You tried to keep your threads nice and tight and yet … What your story probably needs is fresh excitement. Maybe something like:

- Bring on a new and unexpected character
- Spill a secret
- Get a character drunk or furious and have them blab
- *Force majeur*, i.e. an event none of your characters could control, such as flood or bankruptcy
- Let a skeleton rattle out of a closet
- Resurrect a character 'from the dead'
- Get a character pregnant
- Kill or maim someone
- Have a lie believed
- Give a small mistake a huge consequence
- Create a financial nightmare
- Give a secondary character an issue for which a primary character suffers

Whatever you use to tone the muscles of your story, it might be unforeseen or it might be something that the story has been teetering on the brink of – but it happens at the worst possible time. Give your characters hell! That's what you're there for.

Flashbacks

I'd say that flashbacks aren't as much used as they once were. They complicate the storyline and prevent the story from going forward.

To take the place of the flashback, writers often put their characters into conversation, often taking the opportunity to relate the issue from the past to what is going on in the present.

Alternatively they might cover the subject in central character introspection (thoughts).

However, if you still want to use one: a flashback (or analepsis, to give it its posh name) is an interjected scene from a time prior to the point the story has reached. It can be used to give the reader backstory and there are some very good instances of the backstory being used to inform the frontstory, i.e. to gradually reveal crucial events from the past so as to increase tension and mystery or give the reader slap-the-forehead moments as the picture on the jigsaw finally becomes clear.

There's an accepted form of stepping the reader in and out of the flashback. If your main narrative is written in the past tense then you use the pluperfect (also called past perfect) tense. The pluperfect is a cumbersome tense used to refer to events that happen prior to an already past action (are you with me?) and should be used as little as possible. You can identify it by use of the word *had*.

The rule (it's not always possible, but mainly) is to use *had* only in the first sentence that introduces a flashback and not again until the final sentence. The *had* is the moment of passing in and out of the flashback. While within the flashback, use the past tense. This may not work if your flashback is extremely short; you might have no choice but to use *had* in every sentence, in that case. But if you sprinkle *had* uncertainly throughout the flashback it creates a hesitant and clumsy effect.

It's much simpler if you write your story in the present tense – flashbacks are simply in the past tense. (But lots of people don't like books written in the present tense.)

A flashback in a picture story in a comic is often indicated by the normally straight-edged story frames becoming cloud-like in shape and, in an effort to reproduce this dreamy quality to a flashback, some writers like to produce definite links in and out, such as: *she remembered when …* to introduce and *…she shook herself out of her reverie* to close. It gives the impression of a central character day-dreaming the whole flashback.

Are these less-than-subtle devices necessary?

It depends largely upon your target market. I'd suggest that the more contemporary your genre, the less likely it is that you'll need devices to move in and out of flashback – or need flashbacks at all.

Dual time lines

Some books don't merely flash backwards for certain scenes but tell two stories, separated by time, that impact upon one another. The writer has to be deft in interchanging periods, settings and characters.

Q Jessica Chambers:
I am working on a commercial women's fiction novel which follows two family gatherings, one twelve years earlier where a terrible tragedy occurred, and one in the present where the truth finally comes out. To distinguish the two, I am toying with the idea of writing one in the present tense and one in the past, and wondered what your thoughts are on mixing tenses in a novel like this.

A **Susanna Kearsley**, Novelist
Telling two stories in one book is always a challenge. You're very wise, I think, to be seeking a structure that will instantly let the reader know which story is which – avoiding confusion is important, and even more so in a book like yours that will likely use many of the same characters in both the present and the past threads.

This challenge can be met in several ways, depending on the length of the past sequences. Short flashbacks can be set off in italics, or within the narrative itself (a paragraph in pluperfect / perfect past tense sets the flashback up, and then you write the rest in simple past, then slip back into perfect past to signal that you're finishing the flashback and returning to the present). Longer flashbacks of a few pages or more can be given "mini-chapters" of their own, often having a heading that explains the time more clearly, e.g. "Venice, Two Years Earlier." And if you write, as I do, in the first person, you could let the reader know exactly where they are by writing all the past bits in third person. Or you can, as you suggest, trade off the tenses.

I've never done this, but I think it would work well for what you're trying to accomplish in your novel. Charles Dickens alternated between present and past tense in his novel *Bleak House*, considered by many his masterpiece, and Edward Hogan in *Blackmoor* has used the same technique to widespread critical acclaim. So while a lot of people grumble that they don't like reading present tense, I wouldn't let it put you off.

The trick to any novel, any story, is to find the way to tell it most effectively. Sometimes it takes a few tries and false starts before you find the form that suits your novel best, and sometimes that form may seem less than conventional, but a good story well told will win out in the end. Best of luck.
www.susannakearsley.com

Setting

Think of a diamond ring. The setting is at least as important as the diamond – but all eyes are on the glittering stone in the centre.

Without a strong setting, the diamond will be lost.

And without the diamond, the setting has no function.

Wherever you set your book, the readers have to believe in the world you create, the circumstances, tone, mood and atmosphere, as well as the geography of the location.

If you pick a real place as a landscape then research is relatively easy; move your characters to Amarillo, Texas, and you'll find websites crammed with images and guidebooks clamouring to tell you about appearance, tradition and culture. But, just as the images only have a certain depth to them, you might find that your setting lacks conviction. You can easily discover how long it would take to get from the university to the airport and probably what you might see, en route. But not what you'd smell, hear, love or hate.

If you possibly can – go there. Breathe the place in, live it, do some of the things your characters need to do, feel the heat of the sun or the sting of the torrential rain, eat the food, talk to the people, stoke your memory banks. Take loads of pictures. Write a journal. Blog it. (NB The pix and notes are a good idea whenever you visit somewhere new – just in case you might one day want to send your characters there!)

If you write about a real place then some of your readers will know it and be jarred out of the story if you move a flyover or conjure up an underground rail system that doesn't exist. If this is an issue, there's nothing to stop you building a fictitious place that's a lot *like* Amarillo, Texas! You can create another city between it and Dallas if you want the flavour of the place without being bothered with pesky geographical authenticity. You'll have total freedom over the landscape and your characters can visit Amarillo itself, if you want it grounding in reality.

The reader sees your location through the eyes of the viewpoint character(s) so it's a good idea to decide whether that character loves a place or hates it. What is warm and friendly to one could be small-minded and intrusive to another.

Employ all your senses. Don't just mention the colour of the neighbourhood brick and the number of cars on the road; look for telling details, like the local insects that plague you.

Has the place got a characteristic, such as dust or smell from an industry? A landmark building? Do car cars whiz by or crawl in the grip of congestion, at a certain time of day? What's the area like economically? Is there a typical style of dress? As well as what they can see, think of what your characters smell, touch, taste and hear. And their opinions.

Get the weather right for the season as well as the place.

Long descriptive passages are unlikely to be popular in romantic or erotic fiction so think colour, think imagery, simile and metaphor ... but use all that material sparingly.

Jane Jackson, whose books are set in Cornwall
As well as being my home, Cornwall is a never-ending source of inspiration for my writing. An ancient elemental county, it has a rich and vivid history. Having sea on three sides and the river Tamar dividing it from England, it is a place of contrasts: dramatic granite outcrops and craggy cliffs on the north coast; rolling hills, shallow valleys and wooded creeks on the south. In winter, mist-shrouded tors are bleak, treacherous and sepia-toned. But by late spring skylarks sing and buzzards soar above purple heather, yellow gorse and vivid green bracken.

Landscape and weather add depth and drama, perhaps reflecting a character's mood and emotions, or offering contrast. They can also be used to great effect as symbols. Rain, like tears, makes it impossible to see. For one person the open moor offers a sense of freedom, far horizons and limitless possibilities. Another might find that great expanse of sky oppressive and terrifying.

Setting is an integral part of my novels. In trying to create a sense that each story could only have happened in this place at this time to these people, I hope to make it unique – as Cornwall is.

www.janejackson.net

Making your setting work for you
Your setting can have an active role, such as being part of the conflict if you make traversing a crazy mountain pass necessary for your hero's quest. The snow becomes not just crunchy white stuff but a strength-sapping nightmare, thigh-high, clogging,

numbing, preventing machinery from working and transport from running. Life threatening. Your hero might develop a bitter hatred, viewing it as his enemy even if he has spent many happy holidays swishing down mountainsides on jolly red skis.

A cityscape is the mainstay of many a chick lit novel which has potential for nightlife and shopping. But what if the cost of living makes two jobs a grinding necessity? And what if, during the few hours she can snatch, your heroine can hardly sleep for screaming sirens and roaring traffic?

In fact, I don't think it's a bad idea to treat setting as you would another character because it has personality as well as appearance.

And in the same way that you can make characters clash to create tension, you can pit a character against an environment to trigger conflict. A gentle little mouse into prison. A city banker into a cow byre. Throw someone scared of water into the sea; put a claustrophobic into a broken lift; an Australian outbacksman into the streets of New York – oh, sorry, that's been done in Crocodile Dundee. Worked though, didn't it?

Other worldliness

Romantic fiction has expanded: the genres of science fiction, fantasy and paranormal have spawned a following for heroes and heroines inhabiting worlds that exist only in the mind of the writer; strong settings but in which no sense of place can be assumed – yet logic must remain.

Decide that Dran is on a planet that has constant incredible windstorms and you'll have to work out how that affects his power of flight. If Jaxon discovers a secret source of water out in the wastelands of a planet veering too close to its sun, you'll need a substantive reason for it not to have dried up with all the rest.

Fire up your imagination! Conjure up what's so strange but

believable that you will hold your readers enthralled.

Just dodge all the opportunities to trip up.

Avoiding the infodump

Infodump is the term for when a writer goes overboard in setting a scene, usually in exposition rather than through characters' experiences and believable dialogue.

Weave information cunningly into both narrative and dialogue, because few readers enjoy wading through an infodump and it's an invitation for them to put the book down.

Almost worse is spoonfeeding the readers through dialogue:

'Keep down!' hissed Jaxon. 'There's a Roitus from the city of Roit behind that door, a bluish-grey creature with a yellow shell and armed with eight stinging tails, each one bearing enough venom to paralyse a herd of armots, leading to death in around two hours from eventual breakdown of the muscles that control breathing.'

Spoonfeeding is a character explaining a situation in this elaborate and unlikely manner, often to another character who would be expected to have the knowledge in any case. Let your character convey information naturally.

'Keep down!' hissed Jaxon. 'I've seen people die from the sting in a Roitus tail. It's not pretty.'

Combining interior monologue with character action and dialogue is a good way to bring to life your imaginary world.

'Keep down!' hissed Jaxon. 'If that Roitus catches sight of us we've had it.' He took aim at the bluish-grey creature. Each one of its eight stinging tails bore enough venom to paralyse a herd of armot. And it wasn't a pretty way to go.

Creating a world frees you from research or taking photos but for every reader who thinks, 'Two suns, eh, no wonder it's so hot!' there will be more who mentally shred your ideas. *'Why* are there two suns? What's driving it closer to one of them? Does this writer honestly expect us to believe …?'

No. Writers shouldn't *expect* readers to believe. They should *make* them.

Period

Whole categories of the books that come under the romantic fiction umbrella depend upon being other than contemporary in setting. Set in the future, they could be projected forwards thousands of years or only ten. The first two will need you to create a whole new world; for the last you'll have to evolve and develop the present.

But the *writing in period* label is more usually applied to stories set in the past.

The fairly recent past might not be too difficult – after all, if you were a teenager in the eighties then your memory will provide most of what you need – but you do have to get the details right. Like the appropriate technology. Your heroine couldn't just whisk her phone from her pocket to bawl for help when her car broke down but would have to search for a phone box, much more part of the landscape then than now. But so often vandalised when you got there ...

There were mobile phones (the privileged few owned brick-like objects that allowed calls but no texting); such innovations were just breasting the horizon. And now they're lurking, waiting to catch you out with whether they belong in your story or not.

Anita Burgh, novelist:
'Anita, we'd like a novel set in WW2, if you could research it?' my editor asked.

'Easy, don't know about the research – I lived through it,' was my overconfident reply. Memory plays tricks, and even if it is a mere five years ago, you'd be wise to read around the time and check your facts.
www.anitaburgh.com

As well as simple verification of facts you can access the memory banks of other people. Good excuse to chat with your relatives or your mates!

If your book is set prior to living memory then you will have to rely upon research. Don't rely on articles on the internet; get good authoritative books that you can study, or original documents. A book on researching family history might help, as the techniques and sources apply equally to period research.

Efficient research is essential because if you don't know your period you will be found out by readers who do.

Visit museums, enjoy re-enactments, join a re-enactment society, a historical society and watch documentaries. And verify everything possible.

How authentic is **authentic**?

If you're writing a historical novel you are likely to portray history warts and all, with crusty knights and maidens who sweetened their breath with parsley rather than having today's sanitised view on personal hygiene.

For a saga, you'll depict a tin-bath-before-the-fire sort of washing where hot water had to be carried pail by pail and each family member used the same bathwater.

There are also books that are set in period but the writer finds ways to introduce hot baths and plentiful changes of clothes so that today's audiences can believe in the in sensual relationship being a big part of the story.

It's something to be aware of if you write in this captivating area.

Other research

Some writers love research. This can be dangerous! For *Love Writing* I was able to spend a lot of time talking to other writers and reading their articles – and justifiably call it *work*, making it easy to go through the day without actually adding fresh words to my manuscript.

You'll have your own techniques but the golden rules are:

- Go to recognised sources
- Make certain the source is up-to-date.

Gill Sanderson, writer of medical romances for Harlequin Mills & Boon

I've written forty-five Medical Romances in the past twelve years and the only medical qualification I have is a St John's Ambulance Certificate. (Awarded thirty years ago, now lapsed.) But somehow I manage.

You have no medical knowledge and you want to set a book in a hospital, a GP's surgery, a drop-in clinic. Surprisingly, the basic medical information is quite easy to come by. By my desk I have, among others, *Black's Medical Dictionary*, the *Oxford Handbook of General Practice*, *Emergency Care, A textbook for Paramedics* and the *Myles Textbook for Midwives*. These give me technical terms and sufficient accurate information on anything from the early signs of heart disease to how to deliver a baby. All these – and many more – are available from your local library. One thing to remember: be sure that you have the most up-to-date edition. Medicine is changing rapidly. Alternatively, Googling something like 'Injuries to the Brain' will give you access to a vast number of sites. One out of every ten will be useful. A word of caution. If you are setting your book in Britain, make sure you don't use American terms. They can differ in meaning and emphasis.

If you are not a nurse or doctor or medical technician, the hardest part in writing a medical romance is describing the everyday working life. How does a consultant speak to a student nurse? What do staff in an A and E Department talk about when they are having a coffee break? Do staff ever resent the way they are treated by patients – and do they ever do something about it? These are questions not answered in text books. If you have a family member or a friend who is a medical professional – then you are lucky. But otherwise, you have to observe. Next time you call to see your GP, as well as telling her your symptoms, think of her as a human being. Any signs of her home life in the consulting room? How does she get on with the receptionist, the nurse she sends you to see? She's a person just the same as your doctor. Go to any clinic, A and E Department, and just sit and watch. Wander round the corridors of your local hospital (preferably having some good excuse), observe and eavesdrop.

You'll be surprised at what you pick up.

Last of all – you can ask directly. I wrote a book in which the hero possibly had a genetic defect which would make it inadvisable for him to have children. I researched as much as I could and then discovered that the regional centre for the condition was in my home town. I phoned the centre, explained that I was researching for a novel – and was put through to the Director. He spent fifteen minutes talking to me. Sometimes, sheer cheek works.

www.millsandboon.co.uk/authors/GillSanderson

Final chapter(s)

It's amazing how some (wonderful!) writers are able to keep the ending going. Black moment after black moment, more twists than a maze, they thrust their hero and heroine together and yank them apart ... it's riveting!

On the other hand, you get the occasional finale where the fireworks are damp and it spoils what has been a great read. You feel betrayed. You wish you'd never wasted your money or your time on the book and don't follow that author any more.

If you want to write the first kind of ending but are worried that it'll turn out to be the second, don't fret. The right ending for your book does exist and it's already in your mind. It's just a case of recognising it.

Look back at the beginning. What did you want your hero and heroine to learn / find / defend and what did they have to overcome to do that? What obstacles were preventing them being together? What were their internal conflicts? Words such as *resolution* and *conclusion* are associated with endings for good reason. Your ending should answer questions and tie in threads.

But not be forced, not rushed, yet not lingered too long over.

And, nearly always, it needs to be event-based rather than resolved by being talked over. Make your central characters active – don't let someone else come along and solve everything for them. Don't let it all occur off stage and then bring on someone to make a big speech to explain what happened.

Your ending might be Happy Ever After or hopeful or bittersweet or it might leave the readers to their own conclusions. You want your reader to put your book down reluctantly, smiling or sighing, but content.

You might, like an airliner, need a lot of space for your final approach – make sure that you give it to yourself. Don't cheat your reader using hasty contrivances, previously undisclosed facts and secret characters. Some really satisfying endings are circular: an element that was present at the beginning is satisfied at the end, giving readers the feeling that they are leaving by the same door by which they came in.

An ending should have a feeling of inevitability but yet contain surprises. You can draw out the tension by making it look as if everything's going wrong, so completely wrong that it's irretrievable – if you have a great idea as to how to retrieve it! The more courage and fight one or both of your central characters has to display to reach this end, the better. Perch your readers on the edge of their seats as disaster threatens; think big and don't pull punches; plumb not just your heart but the heart of every character on the page.

Wind up in exactly the right place – after the big scene but before you let yourself fall into the trap of remaining with the characters to enjoy the calm after the storm, because it creates anti-climax.

Epilogue

Sometimes, in order to round things out nicely, wallow in a happy ending or find some hope in a less happy one, to leave something open to interpretation or just to have a little joke with the reader, the writer will write an epilogue. It's a final goodbye, normally when all the emotion is out of the way. It can be a punchline.

Congratulations!

You've completed your first draft! *Whoo-hoo!*

Writing a book can be complicated but once you have the first draft down it becomes easier. You have the clay from which to shape your pot.

If you don't have a publishing contract with a delivery deadline, you can take as long as you like about perfecting your book.

Your first step will probably be to read the novel right through – this makes obvious all the puzzles of logic and inconsistencies in character and flow. If you print it off to do this, you'll find that novels read differently from paper than from a screen, giving you fresh perspective.

Some writers scribble all over the manuscript, others attach sticky notes or write comments in a notebook. Then transfer the changes from notes to manuscript – making a separate Version 2 is a good idea to preserve Version 1 in case you find you need to retrace your steps. On rereading, you might see that you've gone up blind alleys, repeated ideas, let the action slow, used unnecessary flashbacks or swathes of description. You are the All Powerful One as far as your book's concerned. Put your characters through the most riveting story that you can concoct.

Because there are an awful lot of good writers out there and not enough publishing contracts to go around.

Self-editing

At some time during your drafting and redrafting process you'll realise that you've sorted out the storyline but style and language could still use some work.

Here are my favourite tips:

Read everything aloud. Repetition jumps out at you if you hear the words in the air, and correct punctuation becomes obvious.

Let a piece of work lie fallow for a while – maybe a month – between drafts and certainly before that vital final polish.

Ask people you trust to read it. Listen to their comments. You're not obliged to act on them but it's sensible to be open to suggestion. And it's good practice for when you're a published writer and your editor sends you pages of "suggestions".)

Don't be embarrassed to use a dictionary and thesaurus. Precision in language is valuable.

Tightening and cutting

If your first draft of a 3000-word chapter is 3800 words, you just have to identify the 800 words that need to be cut. Unless you know they're out of place, don't cut out whole scenes or segments but tighten what you've written. Cut empty phrases such as *There was…*

There was a red car in the lane that honked its horn becomes *A red car in the lane honked its horn.*

Cut weak qualifiers such as *very, quite, rather, some, somewhat, slightly.*

Train yourself to extinguish pet words or phrases such as *suddenly* or *just.*

Don't let your characters begin too many sentences with, *'Well …'* or *'Oh …'* Persuade them not to give the name of everybody they address.

'I saw you, Jess!'

'Yes, I know, Harry.'

Consider whether you really need *he thought* and *she wondered,* which can often be cut if you're firmly in the viewpoint of a certain character. *Would he be there tonight? she wondered* becomes, *Would he be there tonight?*

Don't say the same thing twice.

If your chosen market prefers an informal style, contract: *don't, wouldn't, I'll, it's, who's,* etc.

Write active sentences rather than passive. *Jane prepared the tea* is active. *The tea was prepared by Jane* is passive (and longer). Reserve the passive voice for when another action interrupts. *Tea was being prepared when the phone rang.*

Vivid verbs

Vivid verbs (actional verbs) enliven your work and keep your writing tight by helping to avoid cumbersome adverbs and adjectives.

Let's look at a bland verb:

*Travis **walked** along Main Street.*

This tells us little about Travis, his demeanour or mood. Now try:

Travis walked hurriedly along Main Street.

But a verb (walked) plus an adverb (hurriedly) can usually

be improved upon and shortened by the use of a vivid verb:

Travis dashed along Main Street.

Travis is in a tearing hurry! But you can change the sentence completely by varying the vivid verb:

Travis trudged along Main Street.

Oh dear, Travis, what's up, mate? Tired? Defeated? Sad?

There are A LOT of synonyms for *walk*. For example: hike, hoof it, march, pace, plod, traipse, tramp, trek, trudge, skip, dance, mince, shuffle, sidle, sneak, shimmy, promenade, hurry, bounce, career, sprint, stomp, stroll, saunter, shamble, scurry and stagger.

Each one tells its own story. All will progress Travis up the street. And all are more interesting than "walk".

Grammar? Check. Spelling? Check. Punctuation? Check.

If you're submitting your work, you'll be giving it the best chance if your manuscript preparation is immaculate.

Don't rely on spellchecker – use a dictionary.

Learn to punctuate from a good guide and try and absorb the punctuation in everything you read.

Buy or put on your wish-list a good grammar guide – one that's designed for teenagers or for students learning English as a foreign language is ideal. It won't waste your brainpower using involved explanations that put you off language for life. It just tells you what you need to know in a way that you're likely to understand.

If grammar, spelling or punctuation make you tear your hair then it would be handy for your writing career if you could get help from somebody who has the knack of making the formalities of language behave themselves.

And I'll say this in case you've never heard it: clean your printer head or change the typewriter ribbon to make your print crisp. Use double line-spacing with indented paragraphs;

print on one side of white A4 (letter sized) paper in a plain and clear font size 10-12 point. Number your pages. Don't write on the manuscript.

If you're aware that the publisher you're targeting has its own formatting requirements (even if they don't coincide with my guide, above), do follow them.

What you need

I read an article that declared that to be serious about your writing you MUST have a room of your own, a suitable computer, time, and your family's co-operation in leaving you alone in your refuge. I thought: half the novels in the world wouldn't get written if those things MUST be attained! Some of us have to grab the best that's going. If you want to write, you will.

My study is what was designed to be the smallest bedroom, about 7' x 9', upstairs at the back of my house. The window overlooks the garden but I face the wall. If I faced the window I'd gaze at clouds, birds and trees all day. I have a big desk made by my husband and I keep it covered with stuff so he can't see how much I've battered it. I have an Apple Mac computer and all kinds of other stuff crammed on and around it: printer / scanner, fax / phone (second-hand) with a headset for when I interview people by phone, tray stacks, postal scales, filing cabinets, boxes of envelopes / paper / cartridges and three book cases. And a decent chair and footrest.

There is not enough space considering that I earn my living in here, ten hours a day, five-to-seven days a week.

But, asking around, it seems to me that a study is a luxury. Writers write in sheds, in bed, at the kitchen / dining room table, in the garden, in front of the television, on the train / bus / plane, in their lunch break, in the corner of their bedroom, in libraries or in coffee shops. They write on pads, exercise books, laptops, desktops, typewriters, portable student keyboards, palm computers, with pens, pencils, keyboards and speech recognition software.

Any place is a good place, any way a good way, if you're as comfortable as possible, even if the kids are screaming around your ankles, the phone is ringing or you're being jostled by commuters on the train.

What seems more of an issue is *time* to write. That can be hard to find.

But I have to confess to impatience when people say they have no time to write, but then they tell me everything that's happening in *Coronation Street*. It may be that unless you can give up sleeping you have to give up some television in order to write.

If you have a job, children, partner, parents, siblings, friends and pets all having claims on your time and feel that without your couple of hours of TV each evening you'd just go mad … yes, TV might be your choice. But it is a choice. You could choose writing.

When it really seems too hard

Yes, sometimes writing is hard work. Different writers have different sticking points – some find the first page the most intimidating. Where to start? Just look at how many words there are still to write!

Others get about one-third of the way through and run out of ideas and enthusiasm. They're sick of their characters and realise their idea is stupid / derivative / wrong for the market and they've taken it up a blind alley. They have no appetite for their writing and think it's time to begin another book – and then they go through exactly the same thing again in a few months.

Some writers get nearly to the end and can't handle the

climax.

Or finish the book and can't bring themselves to send it out because they don't think it's good enough.

Others send it out, get a rejection and never send it out again.

If you're reading this segment in the hopes that I have a magic spell that will fix any or all of the above conditions then I'm afraid I'm going to disappoint you. I have done all of the things above apart from the final one. I have never given up.

Maybe I was just born cussed but I simply believe that I'm meant to write. And if I didn't, I'd have to get a proper job. Inspiration is an empty bank account and if I really can't go on at one point of a book, I just go on to another bit. Or I write a short story or an article or part of a serial and then come back to the problem afresh.

But, having dealt with a lot of students and talked to a lot of writers, I do have a few suggestions that might help if writer's block descends on you:

If you can't begin at the beginning, then just write a scene that is going around in your head, one that you know will fit into the book somewhere. You can write the beginning later. I don't think there's a law that says you have to begin on page one.

Bring on an ex-lover, an illegitimate baby or a good rattly skeleton.

When you've written 500 words, give yourself a treat.

If a daily target of 500 or 1000 words is overwhelming, aim for 100 words. Done them? Now do another 100. And another…

Go out with your best writing friend and talk about your book. S/he will *not* think it sounds stupid / derivative or whatever. She'll laugh at the right places or want to know what happens next. Tell her. Go home and write it down, quickly!

Write a few chapters in note form. Or in dialogue only.

Write the end. Write a bit you really want to do. Just write.

Make your writing *me time*, not something on your *to do* list.

Pretend that if you finish this book somebody is going to pay you a lot of money for it. (It might turn out that you're right!)

Stop writing for publication; just write for yourself. Really enjoy it. Revel in it. Then see if you can get it published.

In the worst case, you might have to give up. It might not be you or the book that makes writing impossible – illness, bereavement, injury, marital clashes, business headaches; they stop you writing. If you print your stuff out and put it in a drawer it will almost certainly be there waiting for you whenever you begin to wonder what happened to those people that you used to spend so much time with.

And remember that hardly anybody sells their first book. They have a book they refer to as their first book because it's the first one that got a contract but it's likely they wrote loads before that. My *first* book was actually my eighth – and that's without counting the ones that never got finished.

MARKET STUDY

If you want to have your book published, market study is crucial. There's no substitute for it. Submitting your work without studying the market is like buying a nice plant for your garden and not checking what conditions it needs. The chances of success are low.

Happily, a good starting point is to read a lot. What could be nicer? Haunt your library. Ask for book tokens at Christmas.

Read the books that are being published this year. You won't find a love story that begins with a three-page description of the creases on a farmer's face. Yes, I know Thomas Hardy did it! But that's only a useful study if you're trying to sell your book in 1874. Great though the classics are, and I'm not saying they have nothing to teach a writer, they are not being acquired for publication *now*.

Read in and around the area in which you write. Have an open mind. If you try authors of romantic novels that are new to you, you might find an escalating trend, fall in love with it and find it suits your style. All of those things increase your chances of success.

If you find yourself beginning your book with a gritty, grotty, gruesome murder then your milieu might just prove to be gritty, grotty, gruesome crime novels! (But in crime novels, stakes are often raised by the central character's love being threatened, so crime writers often include an element of romance.)

I have a friend who wanted to write for Mills & Boon and

began by reading 80 of them, across several lines. It gave her a precise idea of where what she wanted to write, fitted. And, yes, she is a current Mills & Boon author.

Once you've identified, roughly, what kind of book you'd like to write, look at the successful authors in that sector. Read their web pages. If you don't have internet access, go to your library and read them there, or get a friend or relative to let you use their computer. Websites can provide valuable insight.

See if the writers have hints or tips, a press kit (as well as biographical detail, this might contain insightful press releases), dates and venues of talks and signings, a chatty blog that illuminates their experiences as a writer. If they offer a newsletter to keep you up-to-date with their new releases, register for it. (If you need anything to practise on, my website is at www.suemoorcroft.com, my blog at http://suemoorcroft.wordpress.com and my newsletter can be read or signed up for at www.suemoorcroft.com/contact.html.)

Read publishers' websites, too. What can you learn from them? Some publishers will have quite comprehensive submission guidelines and you may even be able to make a submission through the website, when the time comes.

Always take the opportunity to visit bookshops and libraries. As well as current books, both will have older books by current authors, read them too, even though they're not being published *now*. Enjoy them but use them mainly as a comparison with what *is* being published now.

Even what's being published now was probably acquired two years ago.

It's not an easy thing to get the right book on the right editor's or agent's desk on the right day and, as the saying goes, a bandwagon sometimes turns out to be a hearse. But if you keep your ear to the ground and your eye on the bookshops, the writing magazines and the book pages in newspapers, you'll soon understand a lot about the publishing world.

Still more information is available to you at conferences and talks and I'm going to discuss them. But, first, let's look at the areas in which you might be writing.

GENRE

When I first began trying to get my work published I failed to realise that, within romantic fiction, there are a lot of genres (categories). Publishers need to know where your book fits on their lists, booksellers need to know where to put your book in their shop, publicists need to understand what they're promoting and all of the above need to know who your reader is.

Your readers need to know if you write the kind of thing they like.

The dividing lines between genres can of course seem blurred but, I hope, if you don't recognise a genre by name, you'll recognise it by description or example.

Chick Lit
A chick lit book is generally written by a woman about a single young woman in a city, its outlook is contemporary and its market is young women. Drink, shopping, men and disasters feature heavily. Labels, names and celebrities tend to be important, too, and cool careers in advertising, publishing, fashion or anything glamorous. The tone is light-hearted, irreverent and contemporary, sex is usually dealt with frankly and although there's almost always a romantic relationship at the centre of the plot, it's by no means the whole thrust of the story.

Chick lit is always heroine-led but even if she begins the book as ditzy and drunk, she will hit a steep growing-up curve during the course of the book. Don't let the humorous treatment mislead you – there are some serious issues involved and some hard lessons learnt. I've heard chick lit dismissed as not about real women but I've read some uncomfortably real themes in this genre. And very recognisable situations! However, no matter how many ordeals the heroine is tortured by, the book is always fun to read.

Chick lit sells well and you'll see loads of big names categorised here.

Generally, covers are bright and colourful, often highly illustrated or cartoonish and the books are around 80,000 to 100,000 words in length, first or third person, often multi-viewpoint.

I first saw it written that chick lit was on its way out in 1993. Has it gone yet? Thought not.

Adele Parks, novelist
According to Wikipedia "Chick lit is a term used to denote genre fiction within women's fiction, written for and marketed to young women, especially single, working women in their twenties and thirties. The genre sells well, chick lit titles topping bestseller lists and the creation of imprints devoted entirely to chick lit. It generally deals with the issues of modern women humorously and lightheartedly."

Other than the "especially single" part, I suppose I have to agree that's a fair summary of my work. Oddly, I find I am agreeing to this strict definition with some reluctance. Why? I'm unsure. I'm ambivalent. Read on …

"Although usually including romantic elements, women's fiction (including chick lit) is generally not considered a direct subcategory of the romance novel genre, because in women's fiction the heroine's relationship with her family or friends may be equally as important as her relationship with the hero."

Ah, then I think I might be slightly outside of the genre if this definition is to be taken literally. The romantic elements (and the exposeé of clichéd romanticism) is essential to my work.

"Chick lit features hip, stylish, career-driven female protagonists, usually in their twenties and thirties. The women featured in these novels may be obsessed with appearance or have a passion for shopping."

Way off the mark for my characters. Many are quite hung up about sex / babies / career / ex-husbands / partners / current husbands / partners but not their appearance or shopping. Plus I think they've all been in their thirties, not younger. Their thirties are great years for a woman – so liberating!

"The setting is generally urban and the plot usually follows the characters' love lives and struggles for professional success (often in the publishing, advertising, public relations, or fashion industry). The style is usually of an airy, irreverent tone and includes frank sexual themes. It frequently makes use of current slang and clichés."

I have had heroines who worked in advertising and television. I've also had city traders, hedge fund managers, mothers, management consultants, photographers, teachers, window dressers, florists and waitresses. I do try to resist cliché.

In summary I think I'm rather more in the genre than out, but I like to shake things up a bit. What self-respecting writer in any genre would be comfortable in resorting to clichés? If I have a problem at all with chick lit then I guess it's that assumption that it is driven by clichés and as such it can't be good writing.

www.adeleparks.com

Romantic comedy

Commonly referred to as *rom com*, it has much in common with chick lit in that it's often marketed at a youngish audience having illustrated / cartoony covers, and the heroine is frequently single, either through inclination, divorce or widowhood.

From the title, you won't be surprised to know that there's a strong central romance and the style of the book is humorous but, again, the issues aren't. Expect to find current slang, language, problems, popular culture, a sometimes self-deprecating humour, a love story that will occasionally make you giggle. Comedy is often situational, although there is room for a good one-liner, so cultivate the ability to see the humour in any situation.

Covers, length and viewpoint are similar to those already mentioned for chick lit.

Many writers find they're moved between the above two categories according to who's writing about them or setting their books on the shelf!

Romance

This is a term as flexible as an Olympic gymnast.

If the book is called a romance then the romance is the mainstay of the story and you might expect to find either hero or heroine on every page, hero and heroine together early in the book and frequently thereafter. The protagonists can be of any age / background / culture. *Romance* is an identifier that's generally misused to cover all of romantic fiction or seen as too general and split into categories.

Category romance is published successfully, and in great numbers, by publishers such as Harlequin Mills & Boon where each category is referred to as a line, and a line may be given one name in the UK and a different one in the US. Each line is identifiable to the reader by cover design.

I'm not going to try and cover individual lines because they change. But these might be typical:

Contemporary – hero-driven. Usually an alpha male, often having fabulous wealth. The heat level can be quite high, the emotion is always intense and the physical attraction towering. Locations include glamorous and exotic.

Contemporary – heroine-driven. A heroine feisty enough to fight her own battles – and to have won them by the end of the book. The reader must like her. The hero may be alpha but realistic. Often sensuous but not explicit.

Medical – romance and drama set against medical community backgrounds and having strong and dedicated heroes and heroines. The romance is driven by the medical careers of the protagonists. The writer must sound authoritative and make the book authentic, so a writer who has a medical background may find themselves at an advantage.

Big, global, romance publishers publish all kinds of other lines such as inspirational, historical, erotic, sensual, futuristic or suspense; you'll find more about each under its individual heading below.

Gill Sanderson, writer of medical romances for Harlequin Mills & Boon

The thing to remember is that you are writing a romance, not a medical treatise. Any details you give must be accurate but they must be subservient to the thrust of the love story. Having said that, a medical background is a potent one in which to set a romance. Hero and heroine are dealing with pain, fear, life, death, and occasionally great joy. Working together they can find a harmony that draws them together. Or they can disagree about a diagnosis or treatment that will drag them apart.
www.millsandboon.co.uk/authors/GillSanderson

Liz Fielding, writer of romances for Harlequin Mills & Boon

Harlequin Mills & Boon were the first publisher to issue "guidelines" to writers regarding length and content of the series they publish. These are not, despite popular myth, a formula. Neither do they issue story outlines to be filled in by a chosen author and common sense will dismiss a "pattern", the requirement for a particular kind of scene by a certain page number. No reader will return again and again to something so predictable. They offer instead a frame and to that extent the guidelines are important; the writer who wishes to be published by HMB needs to study both them – for the basics of length, tone and story content – and the books themselves.

There is no point submitting your 80,000 word sexy romantic thriller as a "Modern", for instance. Or a book centred around home and family to "Medical". Or worse, just sending it to the publisher and asking them to decide where it fits in their publishing programme. No matter how brilliant the plot, how great the writing, the editor whose desk it lands on will know that you have not cared enough, been interested enough in the company or their readers, to find out what they're looking for.

Do not be misled by the shortness of some of the books into thinking that they are short on depth. The pace is fast, the emotional roller-coaster ride of the romance is intense and the characters are three-dimensional, while the range of the books gives the writer wonderful opportunities to develop extraordinary stories which have powerful themes that are of relevance to all women.

For the writer possessing the professionalism to pay attention to the requirements for each individual series, who has read widely across the entire range of the latest books on offer and found the series that has her burning to write, series romance offers great opportunities for publication.

www.lizfielding.com

Historical romance

The popularity of historical romance is sometimes influenced by the period in which the book is set. Regency romances, for example, once popularised by Georgette Heyer, seem to lead the way, although frequently peppered with sex scenes in a way that might give Georgette Heyer an attack of the vapours. The romantic relationship is set vividly in period. Make certain you understand the appropriate history and can convey it through dialogue, introspection and narrative. And without text-book-like infodumps.

The history can be treated in one of two ways:

Not much more than a back drop. The period details are accurate but non-restrictive.

Or so vital that the story wouldn't be able to survive in another time period; the history is almost another character and explores the lives of real people as well as fictitious.

In either style, you need to be able to write with authority.

Inspirational

Contemporary, faith-driven characters and plots, promoting strong family and moral values. Your characters won't have sex before marriage, swear or get violent. While there will be no pre-marital sex, there will be sexual tension. The inspirational label tends to refer specifically to romances amidst mainstream Christianity and both hero and heroine will demonstrate their faith.

As well as whatever romantic conflict you've given your heroine and hero, there will be a spiritual conflict, deeply-felt, ideally preventing your hero and heroine getting together until it's solved, at the end of the book.

Inspirational romance guarantees the reader guilt-free, embarrassment-free, shock-free entertainment; uplifting messages, encouragement, refreshing insights and heartwarming characters. But the reader wants real characters, not cardboard goody-goodies. And inspiration, not preaching. Characters who have wandered away from their faith but find their way back during the story, are popular and as the couple grow closer to their faith, they grow closer to each other.

Sweet

Not necessarily faith-driven but there will be nothing in the story to shock even the highest moral stickler.

The heroine might save herself for marriage, the hero isn't into ravishing. Focus goes on emotion; kisses and embraces are good, wanting is good and waiting is better. Chemistry rather than steamy scenes; leave out the sex but not the sexual tension. Conflict is, as ever, strong.

I write short stories and serials for wholesome magazines and it's really quite straightforward to write romance without sex. If a couple go away together, they occupy separate rooms. Sex isn't the reader's business.

If you think old-fashioned discretion then you'll hit the mark. *Gone With the Wind* has no sex scenes but it's been pretty popular.

Some sweet romances are aimed at the young adult market.

Ethnic romance

I find this one a bit of a damp squib – I mean, we've all got an ethnicity, haven't we? – but some romances are aimed squarely at a particular ethnic group, the one to which the characters belong. If you're not of that ethnic group, you will find success elusive.

Both stereotyping and being overly politically correct are pitfalls to avoid. Simply bunging in the correct skin tone, hair type and slang is insufficient. The reader needs to know and recognise what it's like to walk in the shoes of your characters.

Multicultural or cross-cultural romance

These concern the romance between a hero of one culture / race (or mix) and a heroine of another race (or mix). The central conflict may or may not be concerned with the specific problems encountered in an inter-racial relationship but differences will be there (or why choose these particular characters?)

To bring the characters properly to life you'll need knowledge of the races / cultures involved, traditions and religion, a little about language and a lot about attitude.

As it happens, a question arrived on just this subject:

Q Brona Collins

My hero is black and my heroine is white. It's just a fact. When I imagined his character he was black, I couldn't imagine him any other way. It doesn't really affect the plot except that the heroine is dating someone who breaks the mould of former lovers of hers (who were all white) and her best friend is black and is jealous of the relationship, which she probably wouldn't be were the hero white ... but other than that, if I changed the hero to white, the plot wouldn't significantly change. So the question is "does race matter?" If I mention it, does it have to be significant to the plot (as my tutor insists), or can it just be a by-the-way fact merely to enrich the story and because that's the way I "see" the characters?

A **Georgina Hawtrey-Woore**, Editor, Random House

That is a very interesting question. Have you ever read any Dorothy Koomson? When I first started reading her I hadn't realised the author or her heroines were black. She writes great stories and 'race' doesn't figure in an obvious way. It's there in the jackets in a subtle way but it's a great story she's telling

more than anything. So, I'd say what matters is a good story and if it feels right for the hero to be black, for example, then the story will write itself that way. It's all to do with context. If it's right for the story, it will work. Alternatively the story could be a reflection of the multi-cultural society we now live in and the positives and negatives of that, e.g. how we feel we're multi-cultural but people are all too often confronted by prejudice. *Small Island* by Andrea Levy and similar works spring to mind. In that case race is significant to the plot. Having said all this, if the heroine is dating someone who breaks her usual type, that is going to throw up various issues anyway and, depending on the story, the fact that he's black could be an issue in itself. I'm not sure I've answered this very clearly or helpfully! The answer is probably 'race does matter' whatever we like to think.
www.randomhouse.com

Linda Taylor, author of several mixed-race relationship novels gives this thoughtful response to the same question:
A mixed race relationship was the subject of the first novel I ever submitted and it's the core of the one I'm working on now. In the meantime, I've been compelled to thread these fascinating relationships into my novels where I can. As well as writing about them, I love to read about them. My favourites include the tragic love affair between Daphne and Hari in Paul Scott's *The Raj Quartet*; M.M.Kaye's epic drama *The Far Pavillions* and Lesley Lokko's recent passionate blockbuster, *Sundowners*.

Is love colour blind? We wish it was. We don't want our hero and heroine to be enveloped in a cloud of doom based on ignorant prejudices. We also don't want to tumble into a pit of clichés and, worse, to be thought racist because we've noticed that the hero and heroine are different. But we are writing about life as it is, not as it should be. Can their differences just be a by-the-way fact? No. Because they will not be by-the-way to your characters. Can this factor enrich the story? Yes, definitely! But think about why it's enriching. If you can answer that, you can write your story.

At the heart of your story are two characters. To care about them we have to enter into their minds. You do this by showing us what they say when they are together, by showing us what they think when apart. Both elements are crucial for your reader to get to know them. You may not give both viewpoints, so we may miss the hero's internal monologue, but you should still try to answer questions for both of them. What has formed them? How do they see themselves? What are their aspirations? What hopes have been fulfilled? What, if anything, has been denied them? What makes them happy? Angry? What do they do at Christmas? What was their grandmother's favourite story? How did they feel at their last job interview? What is their unhappiest childhood memory? The best piece of advice their father gave them? Their favourite music track? Who would they most like to meet? Who is their fantasy lover? If you are a white, female writer and your heroine is white, hers will be the easiest answers to imagine. If you can't answer for your hero, talk to people who are similar to him. Are the experiences of your hero and heroine the same? They shouldn't be.

Now ask yourself this. Would your hero have given the same answers if he were in a white skin?

Jaz, my hero in *Beating about the Bush* is a respected CID inspector; the heart of the British white, male establishment. His success in this area does not stop him from agreeing to an arranged marriage as he believes it will suit him and he knows it will please his family. For Jaz to harmonise these elements is a struggle. For my white heroine, Ella, it is a world utterly beyond her ken. Her journey is to learn about him.

151

A hero's skin colour will not, in itself, say anything until an author expands her portrayal of him. Jaz is a British male of Indian descent; from the Punjab, so his family's religion is Sikh and language Punjabi as well as English.

Ella thinks she doesn't have an opinion about 'colour' but she makes assumptions about Jaz from day one. She ponders on Jaz's reasons for joining the police, but is wrong. It was nothing to do with his sense of community, he says, but about wanting to be a cowboy. The most ignorant views of Jaz are expressed near the end of the novel by her father, who simply has no knowledge of anybody like him, and more aggressively by a thug who holds Ella hostage and hurls insults at Jaz while he tries to save her. I addressed these scenes using humour but the reader would be able to discern the unfunniness of these portrayals, too. By this point in the book, Ella has come far in her journey, but she's still travelling. She defends Jaz while realising that she herself is only half-way to understanding the man he is.

Although we have to understand your characters' motivations, your novel does not have to live and breathe a race theme.

Ask yourself why you are compelled to place your heroine in a situation that is unusual for her. Then ask if the themes of your novel and the actions of your secondary characters support your idea. We are speaking in broad brush strokes, here. It would be a bit cheesy to have all your characters experiencing mixed race affairs for the first time, but whatever issues arise from your heroine's experience may resonate with others.

Your characters do not have to see the world the way you do. If all your characters set off flashing enlightened smiles, your readers' eyes will glaze over. You are writing of a black, British man although you don't state his origins. His family background is key to his character, even if he does not let it define him absolutely. His upbringing may seem exactly the same as your heroine's. He may be able to recite from Blue Peter and do a great impersonation of Adam Ant but his sense of his Britishness is likely to be subtly different from hers. Growing up, he is likely to have felt a sense of his own culture infusing with his British identity. It may have been a harmonious blend, or it may have jarred. It may have swung between the two. He may want to break free of 'race' baggage and just get on with his life. Or he may feel like the bridge between the traditions of his culture and the lifestyle that comes with living in Britain. He has a view of himself and you must know what it is before you place him in your story.

You've set up an intriguing premise which, with enough thought, would make a great read. Don't run away from it! Whatever theme or plotline dominates your novel, the dramatic hook of your romance is that your heroine is white and your hero is black. The most interesting line in your question is, 'If I changed the hero to white the plot wouldn't significantly change.' It should. It is not enough to say that your hero 'just happens to be black.' I speak often to a friend of West Indian origin. At one point he said to me, 'I just wish somebody would say, "Actually, I don't know what it's like for you."' It might be helpful if your characters make this the starting point of their journey.

However you approach your romance, it's one that is likely to become more, not less, popular in fiction.

Erotica

Explicit contemporary romances, often between young single heroes and heroines. From sexy and fun to dark and sensual, sometimes adventurous, the relationship will be physical and fully consummated. Settings vary but certainly room for international or exotic.

A story must contain much more than sex. It's about well-developed characters and a strongly plotted romance that just happens to be hot, hot, hot. Tension and suspense work well with erotica and so does dark romance. Some sexual relationships are just full of secrets and kinks and those conflicts are played out in bed but seep into every aspect of everyday life. How careful hero and heroine are of each other's emotional and physical wellbeing needs to be realistic but remember that in an erotic romance, the story has to end well.

Erotic writing can appear in almost any genre – which is why it has its own chapter earlier in the book – but it's the area where, above all others, YOU MUST KNOW YOUR AUDIENCE. The heat level in a story is one of its defining elements and getting it wrong will cause a publisher or agent to return your manuscript pretty smartly.

Peter Freeman writing as Aishling Morgan (and many other pseudonyms)

I write erotica but always having a twist or two, perhaps comic, or horrific, or fantastic, and often with an element of pastiche. I believe that a good erotic story should be more than simply an escalating series of sexual encounters, so for me considerations such as plot, characterisation, research, euphony and subtext are important, not only for their own sake, but because they make the erotic element more powerful. A good example is *Demonic Congress*, which is historical erotica influenced by Sabine Baring-Gould's stories of the West Country. It is set on Dartmoor in the 1760s and I made several field trips before assembling a cast of characters drawn from history, authors as diverse as Jane Austen and George MacDonald Fraser, my imagination and the necessities of plotting. These include six unmarried sisters. The eldest, Sarah, is calm, sensible, kind but stern, beautiful but reserved, and a dominant personality. For the first two thirds of the book she acts as the voice of common sense, patient but frequently disapproving, aloof to the licentious behaviour of her younger siblings. Only then does she get her bare bottom spanked in public, creating a powerfully erotic, shocking scene that also acts as the climax of a subplot. That scene read alone and taken on its own merits would be no more than a spanking scene in an historical setting, although I like to think a good one, but when it comes well into the story, once the reader has come to know Sarah as a person, it achieves real power.

The other thing worth mentioning is that while in an ideal world I would write without limitations to my craft, in practise I work within the moral boundaries set by my publishers and by myself, although as I feel appropriate for fiction rather than as I actually behave, I hasten to add!

I'm an eroticist first and a writer second, so that while I enjoy writing comedy, fantasy and pretty well the full spectrum of literary expression, I need to be able to include unrestrained sex scenes. On the rare occasions I've done otherwise it has always felt like hack work. I've also been involved with the fetish scene for nearly thirty years, which not only provides plenty of background but allows me to gather friends' perspectives on sexual experiences of which I have no first-hand experience. This is invaluable, especially when expressing a female viewpoint, and I've sometimes canvassed a dozen opinions before deciding how to express a character's feelings. (Oh, and if there's one thing I've learnt it's that no two individuals ever see a sexual experience exactly the same way.)

I've published scientific and industrial papers, a few other pieces of factual work, colour text for a role playing game, cartoon strip text, a fair bit of sex related non-fiction and semi-fiction, but erotica is my mainstay. Of the 102 paid writing projects I've completed, over eighty have been erotic novels.

I know it's corny, but if limited to a single piece of advice to a new writer it would be to write from the heart. If erotica is not your metier, if you see it as a way to make money (which it's not!) and above all if you think it's just an easy way to get published, then please don't bother.

Romantic suspense

Combining a burgeoning romance with the familiar themes of thrillers: obsession, abduction, woman in jeopardy, lives in danger. The sizzling romance and the exciting suspense must be firmly bound together and shared by hero and heroine. Think action, escalating tension, startling events, pace, mood, drama. Sometimes you need a larger cast that might otherwise be seen in a romance so that your villain can be one of several characters.

You're likely to have a mystery in your book and a mystery can be enormously exciting fun to write, or it can be a baffling, exasperating flop. (For me: definitely the latter.) Are you good at puzzles? Will you do the research about law or medicine or whatever it is that powers your mystery? Can you identify stories which have strong enough legs to run for an entire book? Can you tangle and untangle threads and tie them up by the end of the book?

The story belongs to the strong, active heroine. As in the name, the romance tends to come before the suspense and the book shouldn't be gory enough to churn your reader's stomach.

Western romance

I can't find a line dedicated to the western romance but, instead, they seem welcome in various categories and for many publishers, especially in the USA. You won't be surprised to hear that they feature all the best of the romanticised wild west: cowboys, sheriffs, rustlers, ranches, saloons, dust, cattle and women who can tough it out with the pioneers. The books tend to be set in the nineteenth century and need historical accuracy, real locations and possibly touch on real events and people. Western towns could be reliant on gold or cattle, anywhere from desert to mountain and although these towns might be difficult to get to, communications made great strides at the end of the century.

Western heroes might have to be lawless and ruthless but they display decency and even vulnerability to the right woman. Can you produce that flavour?

In the same locale and time zone is Native American romance having noble warriors and a fascinating culture. Heroines tend to be those who won't be cowed by boundaries.

Paranormal romance

At conferences and from reading online forums I gain the impression that paranormal romance is rampaging in popularity but mainly in ebooks, where a there's a niche market audience. Vampires, werewolves, shapeshifters et al, the heroes are dark, tortured, sexy, immortal, strong, mysterious or haunted, who have unexpected streaks of tenderness and desire. The dangerous bad boy hero is a long way from the scary animal-like creatures of horror films, though he might give you goosebumps and chills. Isolated by his secrets, he craves love from a woman who doesn't see him as a freak or a beast. Themes of redemption and salvation are popular.

Myths and lore are your research vessels, blended with the most outrageous reaches of your wild imagination and the kind of logic necessary in the worlds of reincarnation, magic, telepathy and telekinesis.

Paranormal romance is often subdivided into vampire, werewolves, shapeshifters, etc.

One of the most intriguing writerly debates to which I've

been party was between a group of writers of paranormal romance: was it more fun to write a vegetarian vampire hero or one who couldn't stand the sight of blood? My imagination was stretched just by the discussion!

Endowing a character with superpowers can be dangerous because you don't want these powers to carry the key to all conflicts (or where is your story?) so you have to give them problems / secrets / obstacles outside of those powers. Or make the central conflict *about* their powers.

The tone of a paranormal romance is often highly contemporary but can be gothic. Or even futuristic. Fantasy futuristic and paranormal romance (FFPR) has a small but growing following. The writers take elements of fantasy and science fiction and whisk them into the mix, proving that the sky isn't the limit. There are no boundaries on the voyages on which you can send your hero and heroine.

Cat Marsters writes paranormal erotic romance
I write erotic romance, which to me means two things: it's got to be hot, and it's got to be a love story. Might sound obvious, but there you go.

There's one thing that's fundamental to writing erotic, and that's that nothing can be gratuitous. It's not porn. Don't just shove a sex scene in because it's been X number of pages without one, or worse, because you think spicing up the book will make for better sales. Sex sells! Well, not necessarily. Readers can tell when you've just shoehorned sex into a story where it's not necessary.

A highly sexual premise helps, which is why paranormal romances are such a good fit with erotics. Think about it: your werewolf who's in heat, your vampire who causes sexual ecstasy by his bite. It also enables you to exclude all those boring but necessary details from real life, such as protection from pregnancy or disease ("It's okay, baby, vampires can't get sick"). I've written courtesan heroines and heroes in need of sexual healing. I've also written a were-cat heroine on heat, who needs sex or she'll die; and an elf hero who has pheromone problems: women keep throwing themselves at him.

You've also got to be comfortable with writing sexy. Erotic romance demands explicit words. There's no soft-focus, and no purple prose. I didn't think I could do it—in fact I was embarrassed just to write the words. I kept thinking my mother would somehow know what I was doing (FYI: she actually does now; we just have an agreement that she won't read it). But the stories I wrote demanded a sexual relationship, so I worked my way up from off-the-page to soft-focus sex. At a friend's recommendation, I read, and wrote, some things that were a bit spicier. Turns out I'm pretty good at it—and these days, I have to monitor my conversations when I meet other erotica writers in a bar, or we make the barstaff drop things. The market varies from highly sensual to pretty damn kinky. Name a (legal) kink, and there's a market for it. Some of the big trends as I write are BDSM (bondage, domination, sado-masochism) gay romance (written about men, but by and for women) and ménage (three or more people). Are you comfortable writing about domination and pleasure / pain? Do you want to write sex scenes between two men? How about group sex? If it leaves you absolutely cold, then my advice is not to. If, however, you're curious, read a bit and see what's out there. You might discover you're really good at it.

www.KateJohnson.co.uk/

www.catmarsters.com

Saga
Associated with sagas are words such as *sweeping, generational, complex, family, regional, heart-warming* and *tear-jerking*. There is

always one or more absorbing love story.

At up to 120,000 words, sagas are big enough for lots of characters and their conflicts, emotions, betrayals, disasters and complex character dynamics. The dynasties and relationships power the story of the traditional family saga as the actions of one character impact instantly on another – in fact, one conflict can yield trauma for everyone! Storylines can be gritty and characters throw themselves on the sword of drama. Or be shoved onto their sword by a villainous character.

Although a family can be a unit, each member of it must be their own unique person. No matter how complex your web of marriages, remarriages and clandestine relationships, make each character and their relationships memorable to the reader. Long-lost family members are characteristic of some sagas, firmly woven into the fabric of the story.

Your characters do enjoy the good times as well as the bad. In fact, the good times make the bad times more acute.

Period can play a great part in a saga and has to be researched and conveyed with accuracy. Rags-to-riches is a popular theme, or the upstairs / downstairs of a long-gone grand household. Situations that are acceptable in society now, such as a man and woman living together and producing children without ever marrying, were sources of bitter conflict sixty, seventy or a hundred years ago and a single woman discovering herself to be pregnant opens up a delicious tangle of prospective plotlines to the saga writer.

Sagas are popular and as the genre seems to be ever-expanding, several generous saga writers have agreed to answer for me what seems to be a very simple question:

Q Phillipa Bowers, novelist:
What IS a saga?

A **Catherine King,** novelist
I write traditional sagas and my stories are based on a model I
have developed from studying classic sagas. Novels that have
influenced me include *Jane Eyre, Tess of the D'Urbervilles* and *Dr
Zhivago*. These books are substantial stories set against a
background of hardship and upheaval. They feature young
vulnerable heroines who are, or become, trapped by their
circumstances. Relationships between the characters in a
traditional saga are complex and there is usually a romance
beset by difficulty. However, classic sagas frequently have
unhappy endings; 'Tess' and 'Zhivago' are examples, so
perhaps 'Jane' is a better model for today's readers. In my view,
today's saga heroine must have a hopeful, but not necessarily
perfect, conclusion to her story.
www.catherineking.co.uk

A **Freda Lightfoot**, novelist
I write multi-viewpoint sagas set either in the Lake District or
Manchester, which have a strong woman as the main character.
My heroine can be found fighting against the poverty of her
surroundings, aspiring to break out of her class and better
herself, or battling against the restrictions and prejudices of the
time. The theme has to be strong and life-changing, dealing
with a serious social issue or situation that is characteristic of
the period, even if she may represent a woman before her time.
The problem might be unemployment, evacuation in wartime
Britain, domestic violence or divorce, parental abuse,
illegitimacy, lost or stolen children, incest, vengeance, or even
murder and prostitution. For some reason, readers seem better
able to deal with these sensitive issues set back in the past. The
distance lends a sense of security from which they can be
considered more objectively while still being relevant for today.
The heroine's ultimate success reflects the Norse and mythical

tenet of any good saga: she must pit good against evil and win through against all odds.

Regional differences are fast disappearing in modern Britain, as are the old industries that created them. I've studied the water industry, hand knitting, sheep farming, the Lakes steamers, travelling theatre, carpet and shoe manufacturing, forestry, and customs and traditions by the score in my books. I often begin by talking to people who are either able to recall such times themselves, or retell the lives led by their own parents. What joy it is to listen to their memories: so real, so personal, so vividly recalled and rarely recorded anywhere else. These stories of the social under-classes, the weavers and land girls, the ordinary farmers and folk of the hills and dales, the oral history of our past, is the life blood of my sagas.
www.fredalightfoot.co.uk

A **Bernardine Kennedy**, novelist
Although the books I write are about families and their problems and therefore fit into the saga genre, they have come under various headings over the years.

They started out under the general heading of 'Women's Fiction'.

Next came 'Contemporary Saga', which was followed closely by 'Misery-Lit', the genre that came into being following the success of the non-fiction Misery Memoirs.

'Gritty Women's Fiction' is an informal description that has been used randomly and probably the one I like best because it gives the reader a clue about what to expect.

I write about modern family relationships, situations and unexpected circumstances that can tear families apart; these include adoption, infidelity abandonment, parental abduction and obsessive relationships, which all sounds rather grim but I always try and add some humour and there is always a resolution. Not always a happy ending as such but I hope a satisfying one.

I guess I take events that happen every day somewhere and turn them into a novel.

www.bernardinekennedy.com

Margaret Kaine, novelist

It was a complete surprise to me when my first novel *Ring of Clay* was described and promoted as a saga. I'd always thought of sagas as sweeping epics describing several generations of a family, their timespan that of several decades, often of the clog and shawl variety. Yet *Ring of Clay* was set in the fifties and sixties, and several of my subsequent novels have spanned less than ten years. But I am regarded as a romantic regional saga writer, and placed firmly by the publishers in that particular slot. So the genre is widening all the time. However, now I love that description. Because I do write about a particular region; I may bring in other locations – *Ribbon of Moonlight* was set partly in Paris – but all of my books are firmly grounded in the Potteries. I also write about relationships within families – and maybe that is the saga connection. A reader at a library talk once said to me, "You write extremely well about ordinary people." I treasure that comment. In my novels I try to describe the emotions, hopes and ambitions, tragedies and disappointments that are a part of most people's lives. And there is always romance. Doesn't everyone long for romance? And the complications it brings provide a rich vein for storytelling. After all, isn't that what the word saga – originally of Scandinavian origin actually means – a tale?

It is also true that sagas remain universally popular. Other publishing trends may come and go, but the saga reader remains faithful. They want to read the social history of a particular era, of the morality and challenges that previous

generations faced. But above all they seek a page-turning story. And as my aim is to write all of these things, then maybe the description is accurate – I have become a saga writer.
www.margaretkaine.com

Historical novel

Many historical novels involve a love story as a substantial thread. The plot is set amidst historical events and characters and will centre upon a historical or fictional character. Based upon considerable research and/or knowledge, standards of accuracy are impressive and the sources of research acknowledged may be as imposing as any learned tome.

Historical novels are often hefty, up to 120,000 words, and readers like to submerge themselves in the history of the time and its realities.

For the writer it's a labour of love to dig out stories that are buried by time and contradictory records, to take a canvas of known events and embroider them with likely explanations and appropriate characters that will, together, form the story. For many of us, history often only becomes meaningful when interpreted for us by a novelist.

Writers tend to specialise in one or two periods. It's a challenge to make yourself an expert on any more. Not just the events and the clothes must be authentic but the dialogue, too. Methinks. Gadzooks.

Retellings

Retelling either fictionalises within a true historical setting or uses minor characters from classic novels and gives them life.

Retelling requires a sound knowledge of the history involved plus an ability to interpret it. Shakespeare made a pretty good use of pre-existent material. (Didn't do him any harm, did it?) As you're putting words into the mouths of existing characters, you have to have a good feel for dialogue and understand the phrases, mores and slang of the day.

Retellings don't have to be romantic but many are.

Amanda Grange, novelist:
I've written getting on for twenty novels and six of them – *Mr Darcy's Diary*, etc – are retellings or sequels to Jane Austen novels. I think a love of the original is necessary in any Austen-related novel because readers are going to be fans of the original, but the books on offer are extremely varied in style and content. My retellings stick very closely to Austen's novels but switch viewpoint to the heroes. In *Mr Darcy, Vampyre,* I did something completely different and wrote a paranormal sequel to *Pride and Prejudice,* but – and this is important in any Austen-related novel – the characters are still recognisable and there are many references to the original. The book says something about the undying nature of literature and the unexpected perils to be overcome in a close relationship. It's also a rollicking good read!

Other notable books in the Austen subgenre are *Mr Darcy Takes a Wife* by Linda Berdoll, which explores the Darcys' physical relationship; *Pride and Prejudice and Zombies* by Seth Grahame-Smith, a surprise hit monster mash-up; *Pride and Prescience* by Carrie A Berbris, a Mr and Mrs Darcy mystery and *Confessions of a Jane Austen Addict* by Laurie Viera Rigler, a time-travelling novel exploring the modern fixation about Austen. The only thing these books have in common – the only thing necessary for writing in the Austen subgenre – is that they are based on Austen's novels or characters.
www.amandagrange.com

And a slightly different slant from:

Juliet Archer, novelist

I'm retelling Jane Austen's novels in a twenty-first-century setting. On the one hand, her timeless characters and plots translate effortlessly into today's world. On the other hand, most of the interaction between hero and heroine has to be rewritten, as they acquire mobile phones, email addresses, jobs and sex lives. If it sounds like a creative writing exercise – 'transport your favourite characters into a different time period' – then it probably should be!

For many readers, the allure of a Jane Austen hero is in the air of mystery that surrounds his innermost thoughts for most of the novel. I want to differentiate my work, however, by getting inside the hero's head. Here Austen provides a starting point, an end point and a few little clues along the way, leaving plenty of scope for creativity in between.

The result, I hope, is an equally irresistible hero, twenty-first-century style. In *The Importance of Being Emma*, shortlisted for the 2009 Melissa Nathan Award for Comedy Romance, Mark Knightley is a successful businessman enjoying an ex-pat lifestyle in India. When he's summoned home for a six-month stint at his father's company, he finds himself mentoring girl-next-door Emma Woodhouse, which has unexpected results. *Persuade M*e has Dr Rick Wentworth, an Australia-based marine biologist turned celebrity author. Back in England on a book tour, he meets Anna Elliot, the girl who broke up with him eight years ago. The words 'forgive and forget' aren't in his vocabulary, but the word 'regret' is definitely in hers.

www.julietarcher.com

Women's fiction

I read this heading and think, 'What *isn't* women's fiction?' I'm sure women read and enjoy every type of book.

As a category, women's fiction is an umbrella term for all kinds of fiction that is marketed to women, the woman is the central character and her emotional development is key. It's a term that's sometimes used to describe fiction that is quite "grown up", concerning relationships and love and a lot of angst.

Having space for a large cast and subplots, women's fiction can be complex. Novels are generally deep on emotion and characterisation; themes are expected to resonate with women readers, to be about women they can recognise in situations that might affect themselves.

There's a lot of freedom in this genre, for the writer – not least to write an ending that's not necessarily happy.

Hen lit / grey lit / matron lit

I have to say that as an author of a couple of books featuring mature heroines, I'm not bowled over by the names given to this category. But people seem to understand them and as the term chick lit is so instantly recognisable, *hen lit*, at least, is inevitable.

The point about this genre is that today's mature women are still young. We don't sit in front of the fire knitting jumpers for the old man, toasting our corned-beef shins and mousily passing the days between babysitting assignments.

At forty, many women are having first babies, beginning new careers, new relationships, learning to scuba dive or parachute. At fifty, they're holding down jobs, climbing trees with grandchildren, buying second homes. At sixty, they're taking the gap years they were too busy to take four decades earlier, shooting off to the continent in camper vans and recruiting energy for a noisy retirement.

And losing loved ones, going through the heartbreak of their children's divorces and helping the grandkids through the broken home syndrome; looking after parents; supporting the male menopause or flailing about in their own; suffering through cancer, chemo and losing their hair.

The novels have contemporary themes, in which romances, burgeoning or failing, often feature. So, if you have a mature heroine jumping the bones of a toyboy after her husband dies and her son takes off for Australia with his backpack in one hand and her erstwhile best friend in the other, battling for her family unit but also for herself – you might be writing hen lit.

Lad lit

The boys' equivalent to chick lit, written about young blokes by men, about love, work and family issues. The central character is often afraid of commitment and self-orientated at the beginning of the book.

The theme can be interpreted that the hero was searching for Ms Right all along but didn't realise. Because he's usually got over his fear of commitment by the end of the book, many of these books have a significant romantic element. At least one lad lit book (by Mike Gayle) has been short-listed for the Romantic Novel of the Year.

Lad lit is big on humour, both situational and one-liners. The delivery often has a "stand up" feel, including swearing, street slang and many references to popular culture.

Do we really need a division between his and her fiction? The publishers think so.

Young adult (YA)

Also referred to as the teens market.

Generally, the single central character is an adolescent and so the storylines concern adolescent experiences, challenges and anxieties. Not surprisingly, these include early romances. That's all experience, challenge and anxiety!

To write for young adults you need to make yourself aware of the market trends and constraints. How much profanity?

How much sex? (I've been surprised!) What messages should you try to get across? The wordcount tends to be low even for novels, and there's a market for novellas and short stories, too. The vocabulary has to be right, you have to understand exactly how edgy it is and you might be required to write as part of a series.

Popular culture is ... well, popular, and your book should reflect teen interest in clothes, music, games consoles and all the other technology that adolescents grow umbilical cords to.

What's noticeable about YA fiction is that it often spans a comparatively brief time and that there aren't that many characters. The central character's choices and decisions drive the story more than external forces.

Make the heroine someone the readers will want as their best friend.

And make the hero someone they will just *want*.

If you're writing YA, your reader is an impatient teenager having a short attention span and a lot of TV to watch – don't waste a page. In fact, don't waste a word. Grip them from the first moment and keep the plot going.

Gillian Philip, writer of young adult fiction

Sex in YA novels is a tricky one. Young adults are sophisticated, critical readers, and talking down to them isn't an option. Even if they don't have direct experience of sex, they're going to have a strong awareness of it. Teenagers can cope with tough emotional conflicts in fiction: it's the stuff of teenage lives.

YA writers are conscious of a sense of responsibility, though. There's a balance between glamorising the negatives – violence, obscenity, underage sex, say – and moralising. Not only will teenagers resent any attempt at a moral message, I don't think moralising has a place in any fiction. Difficult issues do, yes – but for me novels aren't about issues, they're about people. I don't make moral judgements on my characters; they wouldn't let me. Or they wouldn't talk to me if I tried.

There are other considerations for a YA writer than the ultimate intended reader. Firstly there's what the publisher will accept, and further down the line, the opinions of parents and librarians and teachers. It's a fact that a lot of YA fiction is bought by adults for young adults, or that teenagers find it via school libraries, and you have to take that into account. It's not censoring yourself; it's being reasonable and pragmatic.

I've read blatant language and detailed sex scenes in YA novels, but they were there because the narrative needed them. I think that's a positive advantage for YA books over adult ones – in how many adult books are swearing and sex thrown in like punctuation, possibly just to up the word count? In a YA novel you know care and thought has gone into every obscenity, every sexual description, every act of violence.

In both *Bad Faith* and *Crossing The Line*, my two recent novels, my main characters have sex – because that's where their relationships take them, and it wouldn't be credible for them not to have sex. (And hey, they love each other.) Particularly in the case of *Bad Faith* – because the characters are underage – my publisher, editor and I agonised over the episode, but we left it in because it was right for the integrity of the story.

In *Crossing The Line*, my protagonist Nick does a lot of swearing. Well, he would. But I didn't want the book littered with F words, so I compromised on 'feck' – a common enough substitute in real life, not as offensive to parents, but almost as explosive and satisfying as the real thing. For a character who swore less often, I'd probably use the real thing.

Even doing this much soul-searching, YA writers can lose potential readers at the 'filter' stage. *Crossing The Line* was kept out of some schools because it (allegedly) 'encouraged knife

crime'. Now, whoever made the decision hadn't bothered to read or understand the book, but that's the risk you run when there is a filter between you and your readership. Believe me, YA writers are thoughtful and responsible – we have to be – but we also have to stay true to the story.
www.gillianphilip.com

Short stories, serials and novellas
There are a variety of markets for short stories and novellas but not all of them pay much. If anything.

The small press is made up of lots of A5-sized desktop-published magazines and the competition to get stories into them is fierce. However, writing for the small press is often a labour of love rather than a route to riches and you might find the only reward is the kudos of your work being selected and a few free issues.

You will find details of the small press magazines in writing magazines, newsletters, other small press magazines and on the internet. I'm afraid small pressings come and go, so you do need up-to-date information.

The delight of writing for the small press is the room to spread your wings, to push the boundaries, to explore characters and situations. What you're unlikely to succeed with is a she-met-him-and-that-solved-their-problems type romance.

Be original. Perhaps literary. Be unconventional. Not twee.

Websites and anthologies, too, only pay occasionally but there's always going to be prestige in beating off stiff competition. These entries to your writing CV will look good.

If you want to place short stories in a paying market, begin to study the weekly women's magazines, a market also known as *womag* or *magfic*. Magazines pay but the market is shrinking.

But let's not despair. While some magazines have hurled themselves on the sharp rocks of celebrity gossip and scandalous Reader's Own stories, others have increased the amount of fiction they carry and the number of issues published, including seasonal specials. Most of the magazines are paying on publication, now, rather than on acceptance.

So the market is still there, even if it has changed a bit.

Many of the short stories in weekly magazines are relationship-based and quite a number of those relationships are romantic. However, boy-meets-girl is not necessarily the best approach. Finding love is a reasonably durable theme but there seems to me to be a lot of mileage to be had in stories about couples getting over a blip in an existing relationship. The resolution to the problem provides the romance.

Shirley Blair, Fiction Editor, *The People's Friend*
Everyone loves a bit of romance, don't they – and that holds true whether they're sixteen or sixty. That's why *The People's Friend* always includes at least one romance among its weekly variety of short stories, even though our readers are generally of the latter age group! A young romance can take the reader back to the heady time of her own youth. Through it she can recapture those first magical days with the man who became her lifelong partner ... or maybe he didn't! Perhaps what it recalls for her is a relationship that was fleeting but perfect. But in a world that has become harder-edged since her own youth, a romantic story reassures her that love never changes. That's a wonderful knowledge to hold in your heart. But romance isn't only for the young! A mature romance reminds the older single reader that it's a door that's always open. It reminds her and reassures her that mature women can be giddy with new love, too – that just because she's got her bus pass doesn't mean she has to pass up on love. *The People's Friend* prides itself on being a feel-good magazine, and that's why the romantic story is one of the most important elements of our weekly story mix. Yes,

you always know the girl's going to get the guy; but that's precisely why we love them, and, oh, don't we relish observing how it all comes about?

There's nothing more satisfying than reaching that happy ending and feeling yourself breathe a contented "Aahh . . ."

Editors tell me how fatigued they are by shoals of stories about pensioners meeting at tea dances and miraculously forgetting their widowhood and they're firm that readers don't want to be reminded of their arthritis, incontinence and loneliness, uncomfortable realities that may, in any case, already be staring them in their face.

They want bright and vibrant characters that entertain, all age groups, all areas, all walks of life and often having a sense of humour to get them through the hard times.

However, there's one area in which you need to pay due respect to the mature element – your stories need to be wholesome. The women's magazine market harbours almost no sex, violence, profanity, misery, grittiness or hate. The editors don't want to worry their readers. *Downbeat* is a word that figures mainly in their rejection letters; editors buy upbeat stories which have happy or hopeful endings from which readers will get a glow.

An upbeat story doesn't demand conflicts that are minor – it's all to do with how you handle them. Develop the knack of making characters exasperated rather than angry and who react to adversity with fortitude rather than with misery.

If you prefer to write longer fiction, why not try magazine serials? (Although most magazines that carry serials would prefer to know you as a short story writer or novelist before working with you on a serial.) Serials run from two episodes upward. They follow the ethos of the magazine in which they're published and there's a lot of room for character development, relationship and romantic development and subplots.

End each instalment with a curtain – a dramatic moment to create end of chapter tension that makes the readers buy next week's magazine to discover What Happens Next!

When you've studied the magazine and feel you have an idea for the whole serial – resist writing it. There's work to do. You could really waste your time because editors seldom buy serials ready made. The *idea* is crucial. The process is:

Have idea, work up character sketches and general plot.

Ring editor and ask if you can pitch the idea.

Pitch, then discuss pitch, refine, revise. Listen to their advice and take it.

If she likes the idea, the editor will ask to see the first instalment, detailing how many words she wants for each instalment and, possibly, how many instalments.

When the first instalment has been through the editorial assessment system the magazine may buy it. Or the editor may ask for revisions. Or two or three sets of revisions because once the magazine has bought instalment 1, they will want all the others, so they need to get instalment 1 right.

When they've got instalment 1 as they want it they will ask for number 2, probably giving you some editorial direction.

Repeat process until serial is complete. Expect acceptance of each instalment to take weeks or months. Some magazines pay on acceptance of each serial, some at the end.

I have only once written two episodes together and they were the final two, when I felt I was on a roll and the magazine was keen to see the serial finished. Other than that, it has always been a protracted process. But enjoyable.

A couple of magazines publish novellas – sometimes referred to as *cheap paperbacks* – such as *My Weekly Pocket Novels* and *The People's Friend Pocket Novels*. They're great stories, often containing a strong romance between memorable characters, the hero and heroine being in their twenties or thirties, satisfying conclusion essential, good dialogue crucial.

My Weekly Pocket Novels need 30,000 to 35,000 words and *The People's Friend Pocket Novels* more like 50,000. The novellas are on the shelves of major newsagents, just as magazines are. The writer's fee for these little books isn't great but there is added potential as the novella can often be sold, *after* publication (very important, that point!), to a publisher of large print books (mostly bought by libraries, for the visually impaired), which means an additional fee and you'll have a book in the libraries and with online sellers.

But the pay for serials is better and there's exactly the same potential for the subsequent large print sale.

Selling large print rights is relatively simple. Look in your library at some large print books. Note the names of publishers publishing books in similar vein to yours. Get their current contact details from the internet or the *Writer's & Artist's Handbook* or *The Writer's Handbook*.

If you've written a serial, make any necessary revisions now that your readers will no longer be reading chapters at intervals of one week. You might need to massage the flow a little and cut out updates and reminders.

Print out your manuscript, write a business-friendly letter to the large print company explaining that the story has already been published, when and where, any other credentials that make you sound like a wonder-writer, and post it all off to them *with a post-paid self-addressed envelope of sufficient size*. And wait.

Probably for quite a while.

Write something else while you're waiting.

If they say, 'Yes, please!' then expect to sign a contract that will tie up that particular story for about five years.

To return for a moment to short stories, there's quite a good market for the erotic variety. On the internet, you may find that you're writing for recognition rather than for money but print anthologies, such as published by Xcite, are popular. And they pay! They are proving that sex sells, even during hard times.

The writing magazines often carry information on publishers of erotic short stories or novellas and so does the internet.

SO WHERE DO YOU SEND YOUR WORK?

Whether you've written a short story, serial, novella or novel, if you wish it to be published then it's best to know how to select the right victim. I mean target. I mean *market*!

Traditional print publishers

A traditional print publisher is often what we mean when we talk about getting published.

We want to hold the book in our hands, preferably in several formats, smell it, turn the pages and sign our names on the title page. Our hardback or paperback books will be on shelves in high street bookshops, supermarkets, book clubs, bookshops in airports, railway stations and service stations, even some music shops, newsagents and post offices.

Print publishers range from household names to small outfits that put out a few books each year. Although writers seem to aspire automatically to join the largest publishers, where competition may be fiercest but more books are published, the important thing is actually to find the publisher that's right for you and your work.

Although it does generally follow that the largest names come out of the biggest publishing houses, I've read of writers who have been with both large and small publishing houses and have been happier with the small. With a big publisher, possibly part of an even bigger group, they felt themselves to be swallowed up by the corporate machine and coughed out of the other end with a book that achieved disappointing sales. That's a phrase to strike fear into any writer's heart. Now that every shop in the world, seemingly, utilises Electronic Point of Sale (EPOS) – i.e. tills that know what they're selling and computer systems that can compile the records to prove it – publishers can discover how well, or badly, you're doing, by reports from Nielsen Bookscan, the retail sales monitoring service. There is no place to hide.

That's not to say that being with a little publisher will get you greater sales – and your publisher will still have access to Nielsen Bookscan – but you might feel more involved with the process, properly consulted and generally loved. Smaller publishers (often referred to as independents) can see their projects through with great energy and focus and there are many writers who enjoy being a big frog in a small pond.

On the other hand, your large publisher might put their full promotion might behind you and you'll be an instant, overnight success! Even if you take ten years to be an overnight success, it must be a wonderful ride when it happens. You'll see your book cover not only on shelves but on posters, magazine adverts and maybe even television (but not often). Journalists will interview you and you'll be invited to all kinds of publicity events.

This has happened to writers with smaller publishers, of course, especially if the book wins or is short-listed for an award.

But smaller publishers do have to dig deep to find any kind of promo budget at all.

Whichever publisher you might find yourself with, the truth is that you'll probably have to initiate quite a lot of the promo yourself. And it's time consuming. And not everyone likes it.

But let's leave that until later in the book and, for now, just bear in mind that it's tempting to scream, 'Yes *please!*' to any kind of contract but finding the right publisher will make you happiest.

Jane Wenham-Jones, writer

I've been very happy and proud to be with both my publishers and it's been horses for courses – but there are upsides and downsides. With a big publisher, you earn a bigger advance, you have the benefits of a sales and marketing team working for your book, the company has the clout (and budget) to get you into promotions, advertise you, etc., etc. You're given a publicist when your book first comes out, you can waft about parties, saying "I'm with the same publisher as Jilly Cooper, don't you know?" and generally feel very proud of yourself.

But a small publisher has different benefits. Whereas with a big publisher you are likely to start out as the tiniest minnow in a huge fish-filled pond, you may find yourself with top billing at the smaller outfit. You will probably develop a good personal relationship with the boss – I certainly consider the MD of my small publisher a friend – and you may get opportunities you might not have been offered if your stablemates were all household names. For example, I was taken along to a lovely lunch at Bertram's – one of the book wholesalers – by my publisher, who was able to take one author with her. All the others were very well-known indeed – I met Chris Tarrant, Tony Robinson, Michael Dobbs and an actress from EastEnders. I was able to chat to the head of Bertram's and ended up writing a regular column for their magazine. Had I been with one of the major publishing houses for that particular book, I would never have made the guest list.

On the other hand, you have to be prepared to do your own publicity and marketing, be realistic about the fact that most small publishers just don't have the sort of spend available to the big boys. They can't manage the huge discounts demanded by the supermarkets and big chains, and still survive, so there's no point stamping your feet because you're not in the three for two deals. To be honest, although we all might dream of big conglomerates engaged in a fierce bidding war over us, followed by best-sellerdom and being book of the month all along the high street, it's probably best to be pleased to be with a publisher at all.

I know I am.

www.janewenham-jones.com

If you get a contract, you might well get an advance. When I was new to this lark, I thought that the advance came to the writer *as well* as the royalties! Like a Christmas bonus. I was wrong. The full name for an advance is *an advance on royalties* and it means that the publisher won't pay you anything after the advance until you've earned the equivalent royalties. This is called *earning out*.

An advance is meant to get you over the period when you are getting no income from royalties and if you read the daily newspapers you could be forgiven for thinking that every advance ever given began in six-figures. But, no. I'm afraid not. Top earners are top earners in any business and there are some in ours. However, for most of us, advances are dwindling and royalty-only contracts are becoming more common.

Printed books come out in several formats but that doesn't mean to say that your book will see the light of day in all of them. Different publishers have different markets; different books are suited to different formats. A hardback might be your first expectation, then the paperback a nice neat year later. And then you'll be surprised that there's a thing called a C format paperback (also airport book or trade paperback), which is pretty much the hardback with a soft cover on – the hardback in a more portable form – which comes out at the same time as the hardback. But you're more likely to be with an all-paperback house or a publisher that publishes only hardbacks for libraries.

Book clubs have their own formats – generally weight-conscious as the product has to be mailed out to the consumer.

Bewildered, yet? Gives you a headache, doesn't it?

But don't worry, because none of the decisions about format are yours. The publishers will merely advise you what they intend. As with all publisher decisions, you may well be able to influence them when you have bestsellers beneath your (perhaps Gucci) belt or relevant experience to draw upon, but it's unlikely early in your career. It's the publisher's job after all.

It's also their job to worry about the print runs (how many to print) and the greater the number in the run, the cheaper the book is per unit. Except if they don't sell them: then we're back in disappointing sales territory again. And they've made a loss. And they won't be offering for your next book.

Print publishers put money into your book so they have to be pretty confident of getting more money out. Production costs are significant. Distribution costs, too. And if your publisher can't get books into shops – because the big chains and supermarkets can be pretty picky about what they take – then your book, unfortunately, will not sell well, unless you have your own outlets and methods of promotion, which is much more viable in non-fiction than in fiction.

If you have a printed novel to sell, bookshops and supermarkets are king. In fact, they're emperor.

An aspect of print publishing that seems peculiar to it is that if a retailer buys your book and doesn't sell it, that retailer can return it and get a refund. (Returns.) As they seem to be able to do this at almost any old time, the poor writer sometimes finds that some of what is sold on one statement is a return on the next. It moves from the plus column to the minus column.

So, sometimes you think you haven't made disappointing sales – but then you have!

Mad, isn't it?

Epublishers

A comparatively recent entry to the industry, they publish electronically. Your readers buy your book as a download to their computer, or MP3 player or phone or to an electronic reader.

Downloads are increasingly popular and normally cheaper than buying a traditional book. Electronic files can be stored in a waaay smaller physical space than paper books – hundreds on your laptop, for example – making them attractive for travellers. Ebook readers are about the size and weight of a single paperback. But hold about the same number of books as a small bookshop.

No wonder they're being met with mixed reactions – I'm not sure I'd be keen if I were the owner of a bookshop.

At the moment there are various different types of reader and you need to buy the right download format for each. And you have to not mind reading from a screen. And you have to be able to pay for the reader which, at the time of writing, is somewhere between £180 and £300.

Where the electronic publisher is a definite hit for the writer is that their overheads are low compared to those of a print publisher. Yes, the book has to be edited and typeset and a jacket designed, but they don't have to print it out and bind it and transport it by lorry to a warehouse and from there to a shop.

Instead, they sell it from their website and from estores. The customer purchases via their favourite electronic transaction and, magically, the book proliferates as many times as people will buy with a click. It doesn't matter whether the book is downloaded once or a million times because, apart from the running cost of the site, the production cost is the same to the publisher.

This means that epublishers are far more open to niche market books. They don't mind so much that the audience for a certain genre is small because they don't depend upon high volume to make a profit. Their overheads, being smaller, are recouped from fewer sales so they're into profit much earlier than a print book.

Epublishers are good for writers of novels for a small but significant audience, such as paranormals, and also for material that readers might be comfortable buying in privacy, such as erotica. Many paranormals have a high heat level, so they're doubly suitable! Other successes for epublishers where you might find a romantic element include fantasy, science fiction, fables and fairytales, and epublishers, able to take advantage of niche markets, are prepared to take on cross-genre books that print publishers might not feel they can do justice (can't sell enough to make money).

And smaller overheads translate into much larger royalties for the writer.

But I've never heard of a contract for an epublisher attracting an advance. They tend to be royalties-only but paid more swiftly and at shorter intervals than for traditional print books.

Lynne Connolly, novelist

The e-publishing market has changed rapidly over the last five years and it is set to change even faster in the years to come. My first ebook was published in 2002, when it was a minority market, and most publishers thought it was a novelty and wouldn't last long. Now it's a multi-million pound market.

Most epublishers are based in the USA, although they sell internationally by virtue of the medium they publish in, so negotiating territorial rights in contracts doesn't mean a great deal. The model is different, too. The throughput is much faster than in traditional publishing, so that the time from acceptance to publication can be six months or even less. Most authors don't get advances, or only a token advance. Instead, they receive higher royalties, typically in the 35% to 50% gross of cover price range. Unit sales are lower, but the higher royalty means that many e-published authors can earn decent money, comparable to a midlist New York / London published author.

By far the biggest selling genre is erotic romance. However, mainstream romance is catching up, especially as authors are beginning to write for both traditional print publishers and epublishers. As the market expands this will probably increase, as the monthly royalty cheque from the epublisher supplements the lump sums paid as advances by print publishers.

Devices to read ebooks on are coming down in price and becoming more prevalent. Sales are on the increase and every major publisher now has its "digital warehouse".

For the author who aspires to achieve epublishing this means a burgeoning market, having dangers as well as opportunities. Application is made online, usually in the form of a formal query letter with pasted-in partial (synopsis and first three chapters). It's important to follow the publisher's guidelines, and every publisher has its own requirements. Look for the "submissions" page on the publisher's website.

Of publishers whose primary output is ebooks, there are three or four that sell more than all the others but epublishers are a mixed bunch. Some have excellent reputations. Others are startups, which can be of varied quality and may disappear overnight; unit sales are lower, but submissions have a shorter queue and the new author can build her reputation and her platform, as well as gaining valuable experience.

You can do several things to see if an epublisher is right for you.

Check out the website. See how attractive it is, how easy it is to navigate around the site. Read some extracts. Are they grammatically correct and well written? Would you like to read them?

Buy a book. Go through the process as a customer and see how easy it is, and how secure.

Write to several authors with the house and ask them, in confidence, what their experience is of that publisher.

Look at the websites – Preditors and Editors, Absolute Write Water Cooler, Dear Author, EREC (Erotic Romance Epublisher Comparison) and many others that take e-publishing as its subject. Not everything on these websites is gospel – it's important that it's taken in context.

Join the loops associated with the publishers you're interested in, get involved in the community, follow editors, attend conferences and conventions.

Oh yes, and write that good book!

http://homepage.ntlworld.com/lynneconnolly

She's forgotten about Print on Demand!

No, I haven't. Many electronic publishers also make books available to *Print on Demand* (POD). When someone orders the book, it's printed – you might even have seen articles about machines in bookshops that can produce the whole thing in a few minutes. Probably quicker than waiting in the queue to buy a book from the shelf on a busy Saturday!

If you order a POD book from an electronic publisher then it will be mailed out to you. The advantage to the publisher is that because the book isn't created until it's ordered, they never have to store stocks or distribute the product to shops.

Writers often like their electronic books to be available as POD and I can empathise with that. It's one of life's deepest pleasures to be able to hold your book in your hand.

Boundaries blurring

Most print publishers are making their books available both in print and as downloads from their own sites or through estores. I think they've been watching the electronic market for a while and feel it's become interesting enough for them to enter.

And, occasionally, they make some low-demand titles available only on print on demand. Or an electronic publisher will print a number of one title and sell through a warehouse.

The advantage of the technological age is that business models can be mixed and matched and publishers can adapt.

Subsidiary rights

Particularly if you are with a traditional print publisher, they or your agent will try to sell various other rights in your book as well as paperback and hardback rights.

There might be a *large print* edition, which will mainly be sold to the libraries for readers having poor vision. Some publishers put out their own large print edition but it's more likely that the right to publish will go to a large print house, a publisher who specialises in that market, and you and your original publisher will split the fee.

Book club membership has fallen off but is still valuable as, if the *book club edition* manufacturing order is part of the original edition print run, it will lower the per unit cost of production (a long print run works out cheaper per book than a short print run).

Electronic rights – as discussed above. Technology is moving so quickly that this also often encompasses *future rights,* i.e. whatever they invent next. Frankly, I find this a little freaky, but I can see exactly why it's important. Nobody wants to miss out on the next big thing just because the contract wasn't thought out properly.

Other markets (areas of the globe) could be keen to put your books on their shelves, too, some in English and some in translation.

Audio rights will allow an audio company to employ an actor to record a reading of your book, resulting in a CD, tape or download for those who like their fiction to come to them audibly.

It's even possible that your book will be dramatised for film, television, DVD or stage, *option rights*, for set periods of time.

Radio readings.

Condensed books.

Graphic novels (comic strip) sell in some parts of the world.

Serialisation rights allow your work to be serialised in a magazine or newspaper.

In theory, almost any rights in your book could be sold – pictures on T-shirts, computer games, whatever.

Does it affect you, when rights are sold? Yes! Every rights sale should mean money for you and, sometimes, significant sums. How much and to be split how many ways depends upon your contract, which should be very specific in these areas. The advance and royalties on the original edition might only be a small part of your eventual earnings from one book, if the rights sell well.

So if you hear a writer saying, 'The book's gone into Poland, Australia and New Zealand, North America, large print, audio, ebook and it's been optioned for a mini-series on TV!' you'll know why there's such a note of satisfaction in her voice.

The selling of rights is referred to as *exploiting the work* and that always sounds to me like a bad thing. But you can see that it's not.

Magazines

The majority of what has to be said about selling to magazines has already been said under **Short Stories, serials and novellas.**

If your story's sold to a newsstand magazine you'll receive a single fee rather than royalties, either on acceptance or on publication. If it appears in a weekly issue it will be on the shelves for one week only but special issues will be on sale for several weeks and annuals for a couple of months.

I began writing for magazines because I read that having a writing CV that included around twenty short stories in magazines would make me more attractive to a publisher of novels. I had actually sold eighty-seven before I got the magic telephone call but what's the odd sixty-seven stories, here or there? I still enjoy writing for magazines and don't plan to give it up.

Per word, writing for the magazines is not badly paid, especially when compared to writing a novel that gets only a short print run.

You can even sell the same stories in other markets (other countries), so long as you're careful not to tread on anybody's toes. Some magazines are quite informal about accepting your work, whereas others send a proper contract. If they do, do read it. It might affect you selling to those other markets.

If you sell to a magazine, look up their ABC figures (Audit Bureau of Circulations) and that will tell you how many issues are sold per week. If you times this by three, you have an idea of how many readers there are for each copy, because magazines circulate amongst friends, relatives and waiting rooms. So, if the ABC is 330,000 then the actual readership is nearer a million.

A million!

I wonder how many novels get that kind of an audience?

Relationships with editors can be built up and having them

look on you as a regular and reliable contributor is good for your career. Through working for magazines I learnt to take editorial direction, write to length, be part of a brand, write tightly, get the most out of dialogue and give the editor what s/he wants.

The competition is pretty hot – but where isn't it, in publishing?

Magazine market study and submission

Writing for magazines needs a specific approach so I'm dealing with it separately, here.

I always study a new magazine by reading it right through, then listing a) the adverts b) any features c) regular columns.

The advertisements are especially helpful – the advertising companies have spent vast sums of money in identifying who reads the magazine. By studying the adverts, you're getting this information free. If you find disposable nappies, toiletries, cosmetics, bathroom cleaner and a fabric company you get a picture of a homemaker, young mother, a woman who looks after herself. None of the brands are exclusive or designer, she's in an ordinary income bracket. But if you see adverts for exclusive designer brands, private medical insurance, a cruise company and a spa, it's a woman who spends a lot on herself, probably doesn't have to get involved with day-to-day care of any children and household income is in a higher bracket. Study the features and the regulars and they'll tell you if she's interested in celebs or literature, curtain making or Japanese flower arranging, how to look after her legal rights or where to get a tutor for the common entrance exam to a public school. If you keep in mind the profile you come up with, it'll always be helpful in targeting the correct audience.

However, pleasing your reader is an eventual aim. First you have to please the editor. The most important thing is to study the fiction that's already in the magazine. Study content, structure of paragraphs and sentences, vocabulary. The magazine cannot be wrong, the editor cannot be wrong; you will only get published in your chosen publication if you give them what they want. There's no point sending the next *War and Peace* to *The People's Friend*, because that isn't what they publish.

The trap that many fall into, is to think, *I can do better than this*. But what they actually mean is, *This is not quite to my taste and I think I can show them where they're going wrong*. Don't waste your time. To become part of a brand you have to fit in with them, not the reverse. It doesn't mean turning out the same story over and over, it means writing within the constraints and to the word count of the magazine. If that's not for you, then magazine writing might not be for you.

Read quite a few magazines, or, at least, the fiction content, to identify possible markets. *Writers' & Artists' Yearbook* or *The Writer's Handbook* will inform you which magazines do not accept unsolicited fiction. Write to the magazine(s) you decide to target and ask for a copy of their guidelines, sending an A5 post-paid SAE, and the magazine will supply you with a tip sheet, the usefulness of which varies from magazine to magazine.

Having studied the guidelines, you might be outraged to read a story in the magazine that falls outside the stated requirements – well, it's their magazine and they're allowed to do that! That's why studying the fiction is so crucial. But all the other things I've suggested provide good supporting information.

It is normal to send your manuscript (ms) with a front sheet and a brief covering letter. If you have already had stuff published, done well in a competition, etc., you can mention that. (Some writers omit the letter altogether but I think it's polite to send one and helps establish a relationship.) You enclose a post-paid SAE. And then you wait … It can be months.

I always advise people to have more than one ms out, and then the waiting doesn't seem so bad, and neither does the rejection. It's standard, if receiving a rejection, to then send the story out to another magazine, rewriting to fit. Record your submissions so you don't send a story to the same place twice.

And don't be worried if you get rejected – it happens to us all, and it's not personal. Rejections used to really wipe me out. Sometimes I couldn't write for days afterwards. But I got over myself in the end. A rejection just means that the story isn't right for the magazine and they have so many to choose from that they don't need to compromise. Or they might have something similar already in their stock.

The internet

A lot of the fiction opportunities on the internet will get you exposure. Some are paid but most aren't.

Anybody having the time and expertise can set up a website that publishes your stories, so you can see that the quality might be patchy. It's not all bad. But some is. The production might be poor, ditto the editing. You could start a site or a blog yourself if your object is just to get your name out there and you feel you can drive traffic towards your site and at least you'd have control of how your work was reproduced.

I'm going to say a lot more about the internet under **Networking and useful resources**, where it is marvellous. But, as a way of getting published, it might disappoint you if the site doesn't get many hits.

Websites lend themselves most to genres where there's a technologically aware following and an ardent audience or they're attached to an active community.

If your work goes up on a website then you can no longer call it unpublished if you decide to enter it in a competition and if you try and sell it to a magazine you ought to stipulate that you're selling them print rights as electronic rights have already been exercised.

On the other hand, you can have a massive audience! Anybody in this wide world who has an internet connection can enjoy your story. In the jungle, in the desert, in a skyscraper, even on the sea. You could be touching any of those lives.

Competitions, awards and prizes

Opportunities range from short story competitions organised by writers' groups or libraries to huge, prestigious awards with big cash prizes sponsored by big corporations wanting exposure for their household brand.

There are quite a lot of upsides to competitions and I can think of only two downsides, so let's get those out of the way: a) sometimes there's an entry fee – but it pays for the judging and the prize money and tends to be modest b) you won't necessarily win.

Current competitions may be detailed in any of the writing magazines or on the internet. There are various prizes, often cash. Occasionally, the stories of winners and runners-up are collected in an anthology or published in a paper or magazine.

Some people have found their first contract for a novel via a competition, which can be prestigious, especially when promoted by a publisher, daily newspaper, high-circulation magazine or national radio station. Their stated object is to find a new talent – so, it could be you!

Jean Fullerton, novelist

I've been an avid reader of historical fiction since my early teens but only I started writing after attending an NHS management course in 2002 where it was suggested that, in order to relieve workplace stress, participants should take up a hobby. I chose to do something I'd always said I would do one day: write. In 2006 a writer friend suggested that I enter the Harry Bowling Prize. I had read a few of Harry Bowling's books and enjoyed the way he brought the rich character of the East End to life. By great good fortune at that time I was working on a novel – my eighth – that was set in Victorian East London. I sent the required first chapter and synopsis and didn't give it much thought. I knew there would be a great number of talented unpublished authors entering the competition. After sending off my entry, I went on holiday. When I returned I was amazed to find a letter on my mat telling me that I had been shortlisted.

I arrived at the award party and met Laura Longrigg, Harry's agent at MBA Literary Agents, and the other shortlisted authors. At that stage I thought I'd done pretty well to be shortlisted so imagine my surprise when Laura announced I had won! It was one of the very few occasions in my life I was actually speechless. Despite my new shoes pinching like the devil, I walked home on a cloud.

Laura asked to see the whole book and offered to become my agent. She guided me though the process of editing and polishing the novel. In October 2007 she secured a two book deal for me with Orion Publishing.

No Cure for Love, the book that won the 2006 Harry Bowling Prize, was published in December 2008 and the second, *A Glimpse at Happiness*, was published in November 2009. I'm currently working on the third book in my East London Dockland series.

I cannot begin to tell you the incredible difference winning the 2006 Harry Bowling Prize has made to me. It placed my book on the right desk on the right day to be looked at by the right person. It was, quite simply, my big break.

I would encourage anyone, anyone, who is considering entering their book for any competition, to do so.
www.jeanfullerton.com

Once you have a book published you'll find you can enter it into all kinds of awards such as the Romantic Novel of the Year Award, or the Love Story of the Year in the UK or the RITAs in the US. Cash prize or just a trophy, there's a lot of kudos.

That applies to all competition success, even the modest. Wins look good on your writing CV and the bigger wins are great for promo because *Winner of the ...* banners can be added to websites and stickers to books. Journalists and publicists see wins or short listings as a hook: *Prize-winning author says ...* And if they can have a pic of you clasping your glass star or golden statue or whatever, they know it will be attention-grabbing on the page.

Even to be shortlisted for an award is an accolade. Your book will have beaten an awful lot of competition to get that far.

Linda Gillard, novelist
I've had three novels published and two of them (*Emotional Geology* and *Star Gazing*) have been short-listed for five awards, none of which I won. Book awards present wonderful PR opportunities that won't necessarily be grasped by your publisher, so if you exploit its potential, a short-listing can make drastic inroads into your writing time. If you're lucky enough to be short-listed alongside a famous author (in my case Cecelia Ahern for Romantic Novel of the Year in 2009) you'll

find publicity generates itself. It's tougher if the award is for first novels or the short-list includes no celebrity authors. Don't assume, because you're short-listed, that there will be media coverage. *Star Gazing* was short-listed for the UK's first environmental book award, but there was no press coverage of the award and very little online.)

Being short-listed for awards didn't boost my sales significantly. There's usually only a few weeks between the short-listing and the announcement of the winner and it's difficult to organise author events at libraries and bookshops at such short notice. To maximise the benefits of being short-listed you have to know how to use the internet to publicise your book using "viral" marketing techniques, such as Facebook, Twitter and blogs.

Personally, I wish the whole process stopped at the short-list stage! Award ceremonies are stressful, especially if you're not a party person. If you lose, your "failure" is very public and it doesn't matter how many people say it was a wonderful achievement to be short-listed, when they read out someone else's name, you feel like a loser! The more often this happens, the more distressing it can become. Paradoxically, I found the accolade of *Star Gazing* being short-listed twice in 2009 led to a big loss of self-confidence. I felt unable to write in the tired and disappointed aftermath of the award circus. I got very little writing done that year, partly because of the time and energy I invested in PR, but also because I lost focus. When you're trying to immerse yourself in the fragile world of a new book, it's distracting to promote another, one that you perhaps finished writing two years ago.

But the upside of being short-listed is that you'll make contact with a lot of people who have read your book (in my opinion the best thing about being published). A short-listing will bring you into contact with people who are really enthusiastic about books, especially yours. You'll meet, perhaps befriend, other short-listed authors, librarians, booksellers, readers and the indefatigable volunteers who organise the award. Online you might make contacts with book bloggers who will follow your career and keep your books in the public eye long after a winner is announced.

Being short-listed for an award is a time-consuming, exhausting and emotional business but, ultimately, I've found it rewarding – not in terms of sales or my standing in the book world, but because of the people I met, people as passionate about my books as I am. It's worth suffering a bit to have that exhilarating experience and to have your work acknowledged publicly as outstanding. And that's what a short-listing means: your book stood out from the crowd. It still means that, even if you don't win.

www.lindagillard.co.uk

Radio

There are still a few openings for stories on radio – mainly short stories unless you have a published book so good – and mainstream – as to appeal for serialisation. The opportunities on national radio are few but there are local radio and internet radio stations, too. I've even had five of my stories bought, produced and packaged by Short Story Radio for hospital radio stations.

To make a story suitable for radio you need to keep in mind that one actor will be reading your words. One. It's not a play, you don't have a cast, so if you write a story which has dialogue for four characters, a female of 22 from East London and males of 5, 18 and 80 from New York, Tokyo and Aruba, you're making your work hard to select. You can make a greater use of reported speech than you would for the printed page.

Remember, too, that a) listeners may be performing other tasks as they listen b) children might be in the vicinity, even if you think you're writing for adults.

The payment opportunities vary. (That means that some don't pay at all.)

Self-publishing

Self-publishing appeals to some people but is generally accepted as working a lot better for non-fiction than for fiction. So I thought it would be interesting to talk to somebody who has some experience of both.

Marion Fancey used to have a small company that published hobby magazines, so to publish her own novel seemed natural. But the distributor had sold the magazines into the newsagents, leaving Marion to worry only about subscriptions, content and putting the issues together.

Self-publishing her romantic novel, *Ceylonese Sapphire*, has been a whole new experience.

Marion Fancey:

I'm finding the associated things, i.e. planning, designing and creating a website, very time consuming. I've spent the last few months learning a website design program but I've discovered that just putting it on the web doesn't sell the book. So I'm researching Search Engine Optimization to try and improve the situation. Another massively time-consuming job but it will pay dividends.

Then there is the other publicity. I do have a strategy but it all takes so much time to do it thoroughly and at the moment I'm still trying to find that.

And the expense, not to mention finding somewhere to store the books until they're sold (I'm still optimistic).

So I suppose, in a nutshell, anyone thinking of self-

publishing should be sure that, in the worst case scenario, they can afford to write off the amount of money they are about to invest and be sure they have the time to do the PR work. There is a danger of it keeping one from creative writing.
www.emfpublishing.net

If you want to self-publish then you can buy customised packages from companies that will do as much or as little towards the process as you pay for. You can design your package through their website and they have helpful tutorials. They can produce perfectly acceptable books and supply them to your address.

They can sell them from their website, too.

What they can't do is get them into the shops for you.

And you will almost certainly find most bookshops resistant to stocking self-published novels, whereas they will often happily stock non-fiction, especially if they have a local flavour or fill some other niche demand. The exception is if your novel has a link to a place of historic interest or a tourist trap where there's a busy gift shop – you might well get your book stocked there.

Agents

Should you have an agent? It's a perennial question.

There is no one-size-fits-all agent. And if you are approaching certain publishers there simply is no point in having an agent as the publisher has a standard (boilerplate) contract and you have two choices: take it or leave it. Your agent won't be able to negotiate and you'll simply share your earnings with her or him with no reward.

But a stark truth is that many publishers won't accept unagented submissions because they know that the agent won't take on anybody unless they feel confident that they can sell the author's work. So, for those publishers you *do* need an agent!

So let's call her Pandora – because she's the one who left us with hope, isn't she?

Pandora will probably approach more than one publisher on your behalf and will manage any resultant interest. She will know which editors might suit you, who is buying and what they're looking for. For this reason, even if the publisher that is exactly right for you will accept either agented or unagented submissions, you're at an advantage if you have Pandora to whip up interest and cheer your work on.

For many publishers, a contract is still something to be negotiated and Pandora will do that for you; understand the legalese, advise you on rights and royalty rates and generally look after your best interests. It can be extremely useful for you not to have to sully your relationship with your editor by thrashing out the finances yourself! And Pandora may be a tougher negotiator than you are.

Once you're working with your editor, Pandora may fade into the background (perhaps to busy herself selling all the rights in your book) but will step forward to help you smooth over hitches and glitches because an agent works on behalf of the client. Not the publisher.

When your contract comes up for renewal Pandora will look around for the best deal for you. The more you earn, the more she earns.

Have I answered the question? *Should* you have an agent?

Probably I haven't because I don't know you or your work or what's going to happen in the world of publishing. And, if I did, I probably still wouldn't know whether you should have an agent. Lots of writers wouldn't be without one and feel Pandora earns her money by negotiating better contracts than the writer would have done alone and allowing the writer time to write her books. It's true that if you spend three days in contract negotiations then that's three writing days lost.

Other writers say they're very happy to represent themselves, like having control and don't see why they should give somebody 15% of their earnings.

Maybe it depends upon whether you think a contract negotiation would be enormous aggro? Or tremendous fun? Would you be successful? Or miserably incompetent?

One truth about agents that I found unpalatable when I began to look for one: getting an agent is normally no easier than getting a publisher!

Q Marion Fancey
How does one get an agent?

A **Laura Longrigg**, agent, MBA Literary Agents Ltd
- Get hold of a copy of the Writers Handbook. Check out what agents say about submissions policies (or if they refer you to their website, check that out). Follow that carefully – i.e. some agents prefer submissions by post, some by email, some not at all.
- Most agents list their clients – that's a big help because you can see if they are familiar authors to you, you can mention them in your submission letter (you are the agent of … whose writing I much admire so …), you can judge what sort of writing an agency likes working with.
- Always write to a named individual and make sure they do the sort of book you write – i.e. there's no point sending poetry or science fiction to someone if they specifically say they don't do this sort of book. If in doubt, ring the agent – the receptionist will be able to guide you.
- Expect quite a long wait … most agents that I know of take between four and six weeks to respond (you may think that's ridiculously long but I personally get about four

submissions a day).

- If you get a 'positive' rejection – i.e. an agent says helpful things, try and follow up on them. You will have to read the letter / email carefully. Some simply say nice things to balance the fact that they are actually saying no but don't want to be too brutal about it. A typical example: I enjoyed the setting of the novel but didn't think the writing was strong enough. However if an agent says they really like your work, it was a close miss, if they encourage you to send something else, if they give you concrete advice (suggest other agents, or contacting a literary consultancy) it's well worth doing as they suggest.
- If you have had one of these positive rejections, and do as the agent suggests, it is well worth telling them what you have done and if it concerns actual editorial changes, contacting them in due course, saying you have done the work and would they like to see it again? I think if an agent has taken the trouble to give helpful advice, they would be happy to do so. But of course that's not always the case so you need to brace yourself for a rejection, sometimes.
- Above all, don't be put off by rejections – some agents are simply too busy to take on new clients even in the best of times (which these aren't). Keep trying. There are plenty of stories of now well-known writers (JK Rowling, famously) having loads of rejections before finally finding an agent.

www.mbalit.co.uk

Pandora is busy and her first duty is to her existing clients. She will only take on new clients if she really think that she can sell their work – which is what, I suppose, prompts a response that baffles many: 'I liked your work but I didn't fall in love with it.' What they are telling you is that if they're not enthusiastic about your work they won't be able to make the publisher enthusiastic, either.

I have sympathy with this as I hate even having to read a book I don't love. Think how tedious it must be to have to read it, analyse it, make editorial notes, suggest revisions, read it again, perhaps repeat the revision process, then bounce out and urge editors: 'This book is amazing / thrilling / heartrending / hilarious! Do read it!' By that time hating it as much as the dreary classics that I had to laboriously pick apart for English Literature O level.

As well as loving your books, Pandora will normally want to quite like you. It's a relationship that won't prosper if you each leave meetings thinking, 'Yuk!' or 'Grr!' I do know writers who enter meetings thinking, 'I hope she's in a good mood!' and leave with, 'Thank goodness that's over!' Maybe they take the view that it doesn't matter so long as she sells the books and maybe the publishers will be scared to refuse her anything.

Or maybe they think that any agent is better than no agent.

In contrast, I know writers who look upon their agent as a friend, socialise gladly and send gifts at Christmas. I'm sure they must be happier than those who are quaking in their boots.

If you're approaching agents with your carefully polished submission, don't let that prevent you from approaching publishers directly, where appropriate, too. Publishers do buy from direct submissions.

If you get an offer from a publisher, it happens to be a very good time to ask Pandora if she'd like to represent you! She might fall in love with your work if it comes with a publishing contract attached. The relationship gets off to a good start with no agent-led revisions, no rejections from publishers, no feeling from the writer that she ought to be grateful that s/he's got an agent.

Even a publishing contract doesn't guarantee you an agent, though. There may not be enough in the contract to make it worth Pandora's while, she may not work in the area you write, you may not get on together, her client list may be so full that she has no time to spare another writer, she may not have a good working relationship with the publisher you've snagged or she may feel that not even an existing contract is enough to persuade her to work on books she doesn't love.

It's like a marriage. You both have to want it.

If Pandora offers to represent you, it might be on a whole-hearted basis, with a signed agreement outlining what you can each expect, or it might be on an 'I'll try it and see,' basis. The latter is anything other than whole-hearted. Pandora will try the novel on a few publishers and if it doesn't sell she'll shake hands and tell you you're welcome to try another book on her. Sometime.

You might be surprised to discover that this isn't a guarantee that the contract you've fantasised about as you live the cubicle life of your day job will follow. She can't sell every book she handles. That's a stark fact.

Occasionally, you might find that you and Pandora don't share the same vision of your book (she wants you to make changes that you hate). Or that her initial enthusiasm fades sharply when the book doesn't sell. The relationship will disintegrate and Pandora normally sees this before you do.

Pandora isn't duty bound to keep the faith with you when she can't sell your books. She's not paid by some benign charity to keep plugging at your career. It doesn't matter if it's her fault or your fault; if she can't sell your work then she's not getting paid.

Would you work for nothing?

I hear a chorus of howls: 'But I do work for nothing! I write and write!' Yes, but that's for you, not for someone else.

I think it's fair to say that if you get on with Pandora, if she loves your writing and gets you good contracts, then she's worth her weight in gold. But it's not always possible to establish that relationship.

It's a great feeling to have Pandora completely on your side.

NETWORKING AND USEFUL RESOURCES

When I give workshops, I meet a lot of people at an early stage of their writing career. Sometimes they flounder, not knowing where to look for information. Or even that there's any information to look for.

They learnt to write compositions at school and nobody taught them what they might do with them once they'd been written.

The fact is that publishing is like any industry: it has many doors leading to many levels. And every level contains a maze.

But, unlike many industries, it's perfectly possible to self-educate and succeed.

Writing magazines

There are several magazines that come out monthly or quarterly, available on newsagent shelves and/or by subscription, that are packed with information ranging from useful to crucial. Amongst them are *Writers' Forum*, *Writers' News/Writing Magazine*, *The New Writer* and *Mslexia*.

In between the covers you'll find "how to" articles, interviews with new or famous writers, interviews with editors and agents, competitions, market news and advice, competition news, publishing news, advice columns, reviews of books for writers, publishing opportunities and classifieds.

The writing mags put all this stuff in one place so that you don't have to.

A local writing group

A writing group can be wonderful. But you really have to find one that suits you.

What you can expect is to meet up at intervals, workshop, exchange news, cheer one another on and critique each other's work.

It's that last item that can cause issues. Some groups have members who work on the 'Very nice!' principle of never saying anything negative, which, dangerously, can give us the idea that our writing needs no more work. Some, unfortunately, unleash their Rottweiler tendencies and destroy our fragile confidence.

But most see that constructive criticism and justified praise are the only types of feedback that are of any use.

A good writing group can be marvellous. They'll book speakers, hold their own competitions, support one another and pool information. You'll make mates that don't glaze over when you begin to talk about writing, share your problems over recalcitrant characters and holes in the plot and, generally, are on your side.

Simon Whaley, writer, has been chair of a large writing group.
Flirt with other writers on a regular basis! Join a writers' circle or group. Why? Two reasons. Firstly, being with other writers is a great way of sharing ideas and seeking help for problems. Need a hero having a flaw but can't think what the flaw should be? Just ask at the next meeting. Perhaps you have a chapter that doesn't seem quite right and you don't know why. Another circle member may be able to spot what the problem is. Secondly, going to a group is a positive psychological step. It reinforces the fact in your own mind that you are a writer. It boosts your confidence when you realise that there are other writers out there who have all experienced those days when the

words don't flow. Writing can be isolating, but you needn't be alone. They know what you are going through. Going to such a group also sends a signal to friends and family – it tells them, that you are taking your writing seriously.

When I started going to Wrekin Writers, I'd had a few pieces published. Mixing with other writers suddenly gave me more confidence. My productivity increased and six years later I became a full-time writer. And even though the group comprises writers of all abilities and writing interests, I still get a lot from that regular fix of meeting other like-minded individuals.

Be warned though. A writers' group is not a panacea to every writer. All groups differ, so try before you buy. Be prepared to test out a couple of different groups if you can and go to a several meetings to see which one is right for you. You need to pick the one that you feel comfortable with. Find the right group and it could be the start of a long and happy relationship.

www.simonwhaley.co.uk

Courses

Courses come in several forms:

- A weekly evening class, usually for personal development. Possibly run by Adult Learning Services and offering some concessions, likely to be in a school, college, village hall or community centre. Great if you learn well in a classroom environment and having many of the advantages of a writers' group, e.g. networking, common purpose, sharing information, motivation. If the class gels well they might even form a group when the course is over.
- Qualification. Can be full-time but often taken part-time. For example, a Certificate course (equivalent to the first year of a degree) takes two years part-time, probably at a local

university. During the course you'll need to amass a portfolio of work for marking and so need to be able to work at home as well as your weekly tutorials. Highly satisfying, in my experience. Can be taken to Diploma and beyond, if a university near you runs the course.

- Distance learning, either for qualification or for personal development / mentoring (once called a correspondence course) either via email or standard mail. The student will receive course notes to absorb and relevant assignments to complete and return for the tutor's critique. I took a course like this in the early 90s and it helped me get into magazine fiction and now I work as a tutor. You do need to be self-motivating. (Do the assignments and send them back!) There's likely to be a certificate to say you completed the course.

- Residential. You can go away for a week and combine a holiday and courses, typically taking classes in the morning and either writing, attending talks or relaxing in the afternoon. Residential courses can be a lot of fun and you can benefit from tutors who are well-known writers. Friendly and fun, you get networking opportunities as well as top-class tuition. And the more costly tend to be in lovely locations such as Greece, Spain or Italy.

Although many writers have been published after completing a degree or masters in creative writing, this is by no means a requirement.

Alex Brown, novelist
When I first started writing seriously I worked myself into a state about having to learn how to 'write properly', having left school with only two O levels, in, guess what … English Lit and Lang. But I presumed that in order to be any good at something

then I should go to university, so I duly did, and to say that it knocked my confidence would be a gross understatement. The uni in question has an excellent reputation for creative writing courses, but I very quickly realised that 'commercial fiction' wasn't deemed to be 'proper writing'. I took a lot of stick for taking in a book by a very well-known and bestselling commercial women's fiction author, on the second week, where we had to read a section from a book and say why we liked it. Some of the other people in the class (all ages) were pulling faces and sniggering, one even said that she found it tedious and not proper writing, and no wonder books like that never got onto Booker lists, etc. Although she did shut up when I pointed out that the said author had probably sold a million times over the books on the Booker list.

I then went and wrote my first novel, over and over and over, learning as I went and reading lots of writing books. I went on a Cornerstones weekend commercial women's writing course (tutored by Julie Cohen) and I can highly recommend it. I learnt more in that weekend than I did during the entire uni course. Julie showed me everything I needed to get myself on the right track, and then I just kept on and on trying to improve … and I must have, a bit at least, as I was signed by a lovely agent who told me that you can't teach talent.

Conferences

Conferences and residential courses have quite a few similarities: the networking / evenings in the bar …

Conferences can be regional or may have a theme: fiction; non-fiction; genre-orientated. The Romantic Novelists' Association has a brilliant conference every year and I rarely miss one. It's such an opportunity to learn and network. And there's the bar thing …

Typically, at a conference, there will be talks from well-known writers / agents / editors; "how to" writing workshops; group exchanges of information / debates / discussions; talks on promotion, publishing, libraries. And, an incredible opportunity: you can sometimes get one-to-ones with editors and agents in order to pitch your work. Agents and publishers attend conferences keeping their eyes open for new talent.

Networking is an enormous part of what I do – probably because I don't only earn my income from one type of writing, such as novel writing. I have more than one project on the bubble so am always open to interesting conversations that might lead somewhere. Some of the contributions in *Love Writing* came from conference networking – I just collared the speaker at coffee time and asked if they'd contribute. People are amazingly receptive in such a relaxed atmosphere. A quick exchange of email addresses then a polite mail from me a few days after the conference and the job was done.

Then there's the networking done with other delegates, over lunch, a drink or even in the queue for the loo. Shedloads of information about publishers, agents, techniques, libraries, genres, covers, competitions, synopses, submissions and, the buzz on everyone's lips: what's going to be the next big thing? (I've been told it's zombies, by the way, in case you want to pop one in your next novel.)

Some conferences run competitions and award prizes. Winning one of these will look good on your writers' CV.

Conferences require a significant financial investment on your part – although places are occasionally offered as prizes or otherwise assisted – and can cover a weekend or several days or attended on day tickets. The agony, then, is you have to select which day.

A conference is as much a fun experience as a learning opportunity. Often held at universities out of term time, the accommodation is functional rather than luxurious and the cafeteria provides another opportunity to network – in the food queue!

Every writers' conference that I've attended has been a friendly, civilised affair and will almost always provide you with a friend to sit beside, even if you only met them five minutes ago. Books might be on sale at a discount, and you'll often have the opportunity to ask the writer to sign them for you. (Signed books make great birthday presents. If you can bear to give them away.)

And the kitchen parties can be legendary.

Parties and talks

If you meet other writers, you might find yourself invited to useful parties, such as book launches. Book launches sound incredibly glam and some of them probably are. But many are in pubs or bookshops and as soon as you begin to make friends amongst writers you'll find the occasional invite winging your way.

A launch party can be a nice night out with a reading, a glass of wine and another chance to buy a book and get it signed by the author. But it's not unheard of for the other guests to include agents, writers and editors, all very interesting to chat with and possibly make useful contacts amongst.

If you're a member of the Romantic Novelists' Association (details later in this chapter) you'll be able to buy tickets for a couple of parties each year that are wonderful networking opportunities. Agents and editors seem reasonably happy to be accosted over a glass of wine and have books pitched at them. Even if you submit to them sometime later they will be more receptive if you remind them, in the covering letter, that you spoke to them at such-and-such and they agreed to read your submission.

Talks given by publishers and editors at venues such as

libraries and conferences are ideal if you'd like to make contact with the speaker. There's nearly always the opportunity to ask questions and seek advice.

I've said a lot about networking in this chapter
But I really can't overstress its advantages.

I'm afraid that the old saying, 'It's not what you know, it's who you know' has some truth in it. It's not *all* who you know by a loooong way but getting to know people in the industry is definitely a help. Some people hate and abhor networking and say, 'I couldn't do it!' So they decide that they can't be a writer, in that case, and take up marathon running instead (good luck). But there are some points worth making on this subject:

Not every writer networks. Some remain snug in their studies and manage their whole career via email, standard post, video conferencing, fax or telephone. We live in the age of communication, after all.

Networking isn't scary. It generally means having a chat, often with a teacup or a wine glass in your hand. Networking at a party reminds me of being sent on a course when I used to work in a bank. At coffee breaks we'd all enjoy a few minutes to chat about our jobs. Your networking needn't be any more difficult than that. You'll be amazed how you get to know people. Of course, you do get a few networkers who think that it's an extreme sport and make their elbows sharp as they sprint for the speaker at the end of a talk and won't talk to you if you can't do their career any good. But they're few.

I've almost made this point before but it's important. When agents and editors are at a talk, conference or party, they don't mind being approached. In fact, they expect it. I sometimes think they all ought to wear little targets painted on their backs. But it's part of their job and if you open with, 'Hello, I'm Jemima Jane. Could you spare me a minute?' you'll generally be met at least halfway. Make sure you know what you're going to say and say it. 'May I pitch a novel to you? It's a saga of about 100,000 words and set mainly in the Welsh valleys – which is where I live.' You might want to pause for a response there because if they're up to their eyebrows in sagas it's polite to give them the opportunity to say so. Have your "elevator pitch" ready for your next breath. 'The heroine, Tilly, is brought up in poverty but then discovers that her mother used to be a famous music hall singer who has deliberately cut herself off from that world.' They might well ask about your writing CV or some more about the book. They might say that you can send them a submission – or, I'm afraid they might say they don't think the book's for them. It happens! Just say, 'Well, thanks for talking to me,' and go and pitch to someone else.

And I'm going to say again, if networking really isn't for you then stick to postal submissions. Many a writer has found their way via that route. Don't think that if you're not comfortable at talks / conferences / parties that nobody will ever buy your book.

Networking often gives a postal submission a flying start, that's all.

(But if you've got a friend who likes networking then get her or him to pitch it for you! I've done this for someone and the agent said she'd be happy to read the submission. She didn't take the book on but at least he was able to begin his covering letter by saying that he had an introduction.)

Internet communities and forums
It's not called "the Net" for nothing.

Using the internet, you can make useful contacts without ever leaving home. The electronic writing world connects you to networking opportunities, market and industry information, as well as ways of improving writing skills.

An internet community is simply an elastic term to cover any kind of website where the members can interact and speak to one another.

A forum (group) is some method of exchanging information. Often it's via emails that you can have delivered individually or stuck together in one mail once a day, which is called a digest.

A message board runs in threads so if you make a post about a subject you are starting a thread and if others comment or offer information they are responding to the thread. All the postings on a thread will be displayed together.

To join any kind of interactive website is called *subscribing* and leaving it is called *unsubscribing*. To subscribe to a group is normally free.

The great thing about electronic networking is that you need not hang around if you decide you're not keen on a community. You just quietly unsubscribe and go and find another because it's not like attending a class. Nobody will put out a chair for you and then notice if you don't turn up.

I am a member of several forums. Each has a different purpose and every day all kinds of information drops into my inbox. What forums replace in my working life is the gossip around the coffee machine combined with staff meetings and training. Information. Friendship. Contacts. Some of the contributors to this book I have never met but I consider them friends through forum postings.

Where will you find forums suitable for you?

You might begin by looking at the Arts Council-sponsored www.youwriteon.com and the *Getting Started FAQ*, which explains the site, including the message boards. www.youwriteon.com has a facility where you can post your work for feedback from other writers, feeding back on theirs first to earn the credits necessary to get your own writing reviewed. It also has writing tips and links to writing groups, magazines, blogs and websites. You'll find yourself connecting with other writers.

www.youwriteon.com is just one example. There is a huge number of forums and your search engine is your friend – search for "forum writers romantic" or "forum writers romance" or "forum writers erotic" and you get a fine variety to explore. Check whether a forum is global or for a specific country – if you're really only interested in writing for UK publishers you'd be best to find a forum for UK writers. The US market has some specific requirements and the internet is a great place to educate yourself as to what those are.

Just one thing to be wary of – some of the sites where you vote for work you appreciate can be addictive. And voting can be manipulated.

However, being voted to the top of a chart does get the piece of writing in front of an editor, apparently. And I have read that publishers have picked writers up from such sites.

Internet and research

It's really useful to be able to sit at your computer and view areas of the world where you'll never set foot; learn facts; study case histories and garner opinions. The internet is a vast, vast library and if you don't use it you're making your life unnecessarily difficult. Information in every medium is yours for the clicking: photos, videos, panoramas, podcasts and text.

But ... not everything on the internet is correct.

Anyone who has the ability to type and click buttons and tick boxes can post data on a site.

So always corroborate your facts, especially on a *wiki*, which is a co-operative between amateurs and professionals in various fields. Give preference to sites from reputable bodies and those that apply to the appropriate country. There's not much point learning about a medical procedure in the US if it's not done that way in the UK hospital where your poor heroine is hooked up to a drip.

Internet blogs

A blog (short for *web log*) is simply an online journal.

I mention blogs as a resource because you can read blogs from other writers or agents or publishers and pick up inside information. My blog (http://suemoorcroft.wordpress.com) tends to be events based, so if I go to a conference or a book signing or something, I blog about it. But some writers blog about the ins and outs of their careers and it can be illuminating as well as entertaining. Fed-up agents give tips on how not to submit to them and editors advise on making yourself an editor-friendly writer. Even booksellers get in on the act and explain the industry from their perspective.

Reading blogs from the various professionals within publishing is a great way to while away a rainy Sunday. I've even let sunny Sundays go down the pan like that!

Critique services

Essentially, you send in your work for critique. Sometimes these agencies are referred to as *book doctors*.

Some critique services are talent scouts for literary agents and can be a route to a publishing contract.

Details of critique services are found in writing magazines and their prices may be on their websites or they might give you a quote according to the extent of your manuscript. Your money will buy your manuscript a read by an industry professional who will make suggestions and comment upon your book's strengths and weaknesses.

As in any area in which you receive feedback, you need to embrace the idea and look at your work honestly in order to benefit. If they tell you to cut your first three chapters and you respond with a rant about how much your mum liked them, then you're defeating the point of paying for a report. Having said that, you should also remember that the reader will only be making suggestions. The final decision rests with you.

But I'd always advise you to consider feedback using as much clarity and honesty as you can because the fresh pair of eyes that have just read your manuscript will have perceived the book as the reader would – with objectivity that the author can rarely achieve.

Margaret James, writer and partner in StorytrackS
StorytrackS offers honest appraisals of unpublished typescripts – and much more.

Our team of experienced, commercially published and dedicated readers can help improve writing style, content and structure, and give constructive guidance on novels, short stories, books for children and teenagers and non-fiction based on extensive experience and sound market awareness. Three of the team are extensively published in the field of romantic fiction – myself, Trisha Ashley and Marina Oliver.

StorytrackS also has excellent working relationships with many major UK publishing houses, and is in regular touch with many literary agents, so we can recommend or suggest possible markets for almost any kind of book.
www.storytracks.net

Writing coach
A writing coach offers even deeper and more bespoke advice. I asked one to tell us what she could do for a writer.

Kathy Gale, writing coach:
As a writing coach, I offer writers the opportunity to work with me, an experienced publisher and editor.

I offer to read novels and non-fiction works, usually beginning with a sample of up to 15,000 words and then reading more if the author requires it. I give my opinion on the quality of the writing and the potential for publication. After that, if authors require, I can work with them in detail on developing their writing.

As well as advice on publishing and editorial work, I can help with such common pitfalls as writer's block, maintaining confidence, and finding the time and space to write.

I am experienced in and work with crime and thrillers, women's fiction, mind body spirit, personal development, biography and autobiography, memoir, political and business books and more. I am not an expert in children's publishing, although I do work with writing for young adults. Nor am I expert in poetry, professional and academic publishing, screenwriting, and journalism.

Unusually, I offer face-to-face and telephone consultations, which can be much better for the author than written reports alone, as they are able to ask any questions they may have, enter into a dialogue about their work and get to know their writing coach, which can be a highly supportive experience.

It is important to my work that I have a background in book publishing – I have worked as senior editor and director of several leading publishing houses over a long career and I remain in publishing at a senior level. This keeps me up-to-date with the ever-changing world of publishing and aware of what publishers are looking for.

www.kgpublishingservices.co.uk

Literature development
Your literature development worker is a hub, the point of contact for literature in your area and a bridge between it and other art forms such as drama, dance and visual arts, and also

education, offering writers the benefit of experience and advising them how to maximise their opportunities.

You may have a Literature Development Officer or an Arts Officer, depending where you live and where the literature worker gets their funding. It might be a full-time or a part-time post. Some literature workers are writers, too, so really understand what you need. But he or she is there to put you in touch with writers' groups, signpost suitable courses and provide pertinent information. If you win a competition or gain success your work can be publicised on the literature worker's newsletter and website or introduced to a relevant critiquing service and/or mentor. And then there's support and encouragement – we all need it.

If you're published, publicity might be available on a wider network, regional or national. You can be recommended for events and festivals and, of course, library events, writers' groups, schools and colleges and be used as a competition judge, tutor or mentor. In some form – website, blog or pages on the website of their funding body – your literature worker will maintain an internet presence that is a central resource for writers in the area, containing contacts with the local press, information on training and feedback, links to other relevant websites, local, regional and national literature organisations, and funding. It will probably give you an idea of how that literature officer sees their role in enriching the quality and diversity of literature.

There may be a newsletter – easy to disseminate widely in this electronic age – information-heavy containing writers' opportunities and events. Databases might also be compiled to benefit those looking for writers for classes, festivals or talks.

Your literature worker will probably have a background in publishing or literature, be used to making opportunities, might be preoccupied with funding and the state of affairs at Arts

Council England, and yet remain enthusiastic.

Look for information on your council's website or phone them. Your librarian will certainly have the contact details, too. Do an internet search for *Literature Development* and your county or area. For instance, a search for *Literature Development Scotland* returns over two million results and *Literature Development Cardiff* over one hundred thousand.

Be prepared to be pro-active and contact the Literature Development Officer or Arts Officer – don't wait for them to stumble upon you and winkle you out of your shell. It's a mutual relationship and one that can be built upon, the literature worker working with all levels of writer, helping them, and helping them to help others.

Writers need to generate income and develop audiences. A literature worker can fight the corner for literature and focus on people getting paid – trying to alter the view, apparently held by many, that writing is just something done in one's spare time.

Who are literature workers here for?

Novelists, poets, playwrights, scriptwriters, writer / performers, hobby writers, new writers, published writers, librarians, promoters, festival organisers, writers' groups, book groups, writing course providers, educational institutions, all media, organisations in health and social cohesion that might employ writers, readers and audiences.

And you.

Romantic Novelists' Association

An association based in the UK that will accept members from around the world, although it is most useful regarding the UK market. It exists to promote romantic fiction and provide services to its members.

The Association is fifty years old now so it's obviously

working pretty well.

I've been a member since about 1998 and was on the committee for some years. The support that the RNA gave to me was a huge help towards getting my first novel published and many of my writing friends and contacts are RNA members. Some of the bestselling writers of romantic and erotic fiction are members and whenever you're at an RNA event you're amongst friends.

As well as their excellent annual conference and a couple of parties a year, the Association puts on helpful meetings which have speakers from the industry and great networking opportunities (no, I'm not going to shut up about networking). There are also occasional educational seminars and industry days.

Local chapters all around the UK organise informal lunches or formal meetings which have speakers. There's also an email forum for the exchange of all news and views writing-related.

But perhaps one of the RNA's greatest strengths is its New Writers' Scheme. Writers who have not qualified for full membership by having a suitable novel published may join the Association as a New Writer. This involves a greater fee than for full membership and allows the writer to submit one manuscript a year for critique by one of the published writers in a similar field. But it's a *bargain*.

The top few manuscripts are given a second read by another reader and if thought to be of publishable quality the Scheme Coordinator will introduce the writer to a suitable agent or publisher.

(Tip: there are only 250 of these places each year so join in January to avoid disappointment!)

New Writers have most of the benefits of full members other than voting rights at the Annual General Meeting.

The RNA runs or administers several awards, such as (at

time of writing) the Romantic Novel of the Year Award; the Love Story of the Year; the New Writers' Award; Elizabeth Goudge Trophy and the Katie Fforde Bursary Award.

Members receive a copy of the Association magazine, *Romance Matters*, four times a year, to celebrate its fiftieth anniversary the Association published its history and also *Loves Me, Loves Me Not*, an anthology of short stories, of which I was an editor. (Picture me looking proud.)
www.rna-uk.org

Romance Writers of America

The RWA is much larger than the RNA but has similar aims and functions. It supports members in their writing careers and, although a significant portion of its membership lives outside the US, it is orientated towards being published in North America.

The RWA's conference is *huge!* I must go, soon.

The RITA Awards and the Golden Heart Awards are sponsored by the RWA and if you're published in North America then membership is a great benefit. They, too, have many local chapters and their own magazine.
www.rwanational.org

You won't be surprised to know that there's also the *Romance Writers of Australia* www.romanceaustralia.com and *Romance Writers of New Zealand* www.romancewriters.co.nz.

GETTING DOWN TO BUSINESS

OK, so you've written a brilliant romantic novel and now you'd like others to be able to read it.

You need a publisher.

And a publisher is unlikely to put your book out there unless they can make money from it – which means you should make some money from it, too. How much? It could be almost anything, from pence to millions of pounds. But here's a hint: many writers do things other than writing to make money. I certainly do! I teach creative writing, appraise manuscripts and judge competitions, almost anything that is to do with writing but will bring in income.

Many writers have a day job, although it might be part-time.

But however much money you eventually make from your writing, the way you go about it doesn't vary.

Q Marion Fancey
How does one get published?

A **Laura Longrigg**, agent, MBA Literary Agents Ltd
Get an agent is the best advice anyone could give you, I think.

However, there are certain books which don't need agenting quite as much as others. Children's is one area where you can go to a publisher having an idea and some illustrations and if they can see signs of real talent they may well work with you directly, commissioning work from you.

Academic work doesn't need an agent, partly because if you

are in this world, you know who the right editors are for your particular field, or are asked to write things. Partly because the pay is pretty awful so you don't need to share it with an agent … I would include educational writing in this bracket, too. Illustrated books … like children's, you can often approach publishers directly about ideas.

But in all cases, an agent is quite a help when it comes to contracts / negotiating money. On the other hand, you can talk to the Society of Authors (if you are a member) who are great for problem solving and talking through worries.

To get a publisher's attention – to be the sort of person that publishers actively seek out it is very helpful to:

- be a journalist, print or other media. Publishers often assume you have a book in you, as, to be fair, do a lot of journalists themselves.
- be a prize winner – there are many, many literary prizes to be won, some regional, some specialist, but all look great on the CV and will make a publisher take notice.
- be a short story writer – again, like journalists, it's assumed you have a book in you.
- have done a creative writing course at university level. There are all sorts of shapes and sizes of these, of course, and some are more prestigious than others. And you should definitely check out the tutors, some of whom have much better reputations than others. But, of course, it shows you are serious about your writing and want to get better at it.
- have done something eye-catching – whether it is have a terrible childhood, have walked barefoot to the North Pole, made several million before you are twenty, invented the latest eco friendly planet saving gizmo … In other words you are the story. (In this instance you will probably need a ghostwriter, but that's a whole other area and of course one that publishers are very used to.)

- have friends in the business (not entirely joking!)
www.mbalit.co.uk

What does a publisher or agent want?
Pandora, the agent, or an editor – let's call him Timothy – want a fantastic book that they can sell and which will make everyone concerned a lot of dosh. To rouse their interest you need to present them with a submission package that's as professional as you can make it. Think of your manuscript as a candidate for a job interview: ensure it arrives having tidy hair and shiny shoes.

If you know that your spelling, punctuation or grammar isn't great then either brush it up or enlist the help of someone who has the necessary skills. It's worth taking pains because you're presenting your work to somebody who works with language.

Use a sensible font and make sure your manner of printing is clean and clear. Print on one side of white A4 paper. Number the pages. Include a cover sheet which has your details on. Put a rubber band around your submission, don't attach with pins or staples. There's really no need for a folder and using a ring binder ... well, you're showing your inexperience.

Read up on what the Pandora or Timothy wants in *Writers' & Artists Yearbook* or *The Writer's Handbook*, but your submission will normally include:

The first three chapters of your book
Normally amounting to no more than 100 pages. I honestly have heard of a writer who simply made her whole manuscript three very long chapters and sent that. That book was rejected. I should imagine Timothy rolled his eyes a bit.

Yes, they really do want the first three chapters. They want to see how your book opens and whether it will retain reader interest. If you send chapters 4, 5 and 6 because you think they're the best, Timothy will just wonder why you haven't written the whole book to that standard.

And chapters 4, 9 and 23 will be equally unhelpful.

Synopsis

Do you know anybody who likes writing synopses? No, I don't. I always feel like saying that if I could boil my book down to its bare bones of about 200 words then I wouldn't have written the other 80,000 in the first place. (I never *actually* say that, obviously!) And I always have an uncomfortable feeling that my synopsis makes my book sound no good.

But, as it plays a really important part in your submission package, your synopsis deserves all the time, consideration and sweat that you can lavish on it and you should see it as your opportunity to sell your book to Timothy or Pandora in exactly the same way that your publisher will see the blurb on the back of a book as a major opportunity to turn a browser into a buyer.

The synopsis allows Pandora or Timothy to see whether, if they're interested in the first three chapters, the rest of the story is promising. Is the number of characters right? Is the storyline focused? Is there a terrific ending?

A synopsis is written using broad brush-strokes and concerns the whole story, including chapters 1 to 3, including the ending, using memorable words and descriptions that add drama. Its job is to bring your book to life so that Timothy and Pandora want to read more.

Try beginning with a single sentence that sums up the theme of the book, then a second covering what kind of novel it is and where it's set. Move on to major characters, their motivations and how one character's actions impacts upon another character. Pick out highspots, or plotpoints on which the story pivots – crisis, obstacle, joyous resolution. Add a sprinkling of setting and atmosphere. At this time, the synopsis is probably pretty badly written but contains every element it needs.

Bring on the two e's – emotion and enthusiasm.

If you've explained that Shelli's received a letter from the sister she thought dead, include how that made her feel and how that feeling made her act. *Shelli is so shocked to receive a letter from Ellie, the sister who died three years ago, that she bursts in on Ellie's husband ...* Emotion is often synonymous with character motivation.

But enthusiasm? That has to be yours.

Pretend that you've just read your book for the first time, you love it and you're falling over yourself to tell a friend. Try and make her want to read it, too! A hooky first paragraph, a synopsis crammed with conflicts and resolutions for the fascinating major characters. Fizz with excitement over the central romance. And wherever you might be tempted to refer to *the book* or *the novel*, use the book's title, instead.

But leave out all the, 'You really must read this book! It's FAB!' stuff, obviously.

A synopsis is often only one or two pages and is written in the present tense, third person, in the same tone as the book. Remember vivid verbs; be ruthless in chopping out adverbs, adjectives and passive sentences.

Covering letter

Your covering letter is your introduction to Pandora or Timothy. Be business friendly and use appropriate language – not fawning or familiar but not taking refuge in office-speak; especially outmoded office-speak.

A covering letter need be only three paragraphs:

1. You are submitting the first three chapters and synopsis of your book, *The Best Romance Ever* – why

to this editor or agent? Have you met them? Heard them speak? Have you an introduction from an appropriate person? Do you feel that they represent similar writers?

2. Sum up the plot in three sentences, a good and succinct description. Who will the book appeal to? (Hint: make them sound like book buyers!) What sort of novel is it? Are there unique selling points? Are you taking a fresh look at multicultural relationships or the dangers of a wild affair? Is the book topical? Are there any particular promotional opportunities you envisage? Something special that readers will get from your book?

3. Your publishing history (if you have one) or writing qualifications (if you have any). Include competition successes. Is there something that qualifies you to write this book? (If it concerns a diamond heist and you've been present during a robbery, for example. Or if you've shared the heroine's career choices or have other relevant expertise or knowledge.) Your day job (if you have one). Thank them for taking time to read your submission.

Don't make your letter a plea! Don't sound desperate or be grateful. Be factual and clear but be yourself. Don't tell any lies but make the truth sound good.

Things not to include:
My mum / best friend thinks this book is as good as anything published.
   I'd like to offer you the honour of publishing my work.
   I won an essay prize in 1989.
   A catalogue of sentences beginning, 'I ...'
   Circumspect language: 'I hope ... probably ... maybe ...'

Archaic office-speak: '... much obliged ... beg to ... your servant ...'

Be prepared to wait for a response. You've just approached a busy person, unasked, and you'll give yourself the best chance by being polite and patient.

To write your novel is a creative act. To submit it is strictly business.

Caroline Sheldon, Caroline Sheldon Literary Agency

We are looking for fiction combining great writing with fantastic storytelling. We also like things that are of the moment.

Alongside writing a terrifically good book, I would advise writers to make sure they present themselves as well as they possibly can in the covering letter they send in with the submission. Things that put us off are:

- Single spaced manuscripts in tiddly or faded type or fancy fonts (you should always double space).
- Lacklustre submission letters which have little information.
- Proposals for fictional novels (what other sort are there?)
- Non-consecutive chapters e.g. 1, 13 and 26 (always send the first three; if you're not confident in them you shouldn't be sending them out).
- Humorous submissions which aren't funny.
- String, rusty paperclips, treasury tags, too much Sellotape and the like.
- Undersize envelopes, unstamped envelopes, international reply coupons.
- Absence of contact information and undated letters.
- Submission letters that say your mum loved it.
- Email submissions to more than one agent – plump for Caroline or Penny.

www.carolinesheldon.co.uk

Q Marion Fancey
How does one know if one's work is good enough?

A **Melanie Hilton**, New Writers' Co-ordinator of the Romantic Novelist's Association's New Writers' Scheme, who writes for Mills & Boon Historical as Louise Allen
Now that's a tough question, and one that even published authors who have many books behind them worry about.

Learning to judge one's own work takes time and experience and even then it is sometimes difficult to be completely objective about what is working and what isn't. Listen to your instincts – if you are uneasy about something – whether it is a phrase or a character, stop and pay attention to that inner voice. Learn to set work aside "to settle" and come back to it with the benefit of some distance.

Seeking honest and informed feedback is essential. Unfortunately, this doesn't mean listening just to your mum or your best friend – they'll love it whatever its faults! One of the best sources of detailed and honest feedback is the Romantic Novelists' Association's New Writers' Scheme.

Wherever you get your feedback from, the next skill to learn is how to accept it, because even the most constructive comments can feel like a personal attack. Try and distance yourself from the book, look dispassionately at what is being said, then make a personal decision on whether you are going to accept that piece of criticism or not.

And then there is the question – good enough for what? A piece of good writing may not be commercially successful for a number of reasons, so study the market you are aiming at carefully. And, good luck!
www.louiseallenregency.co.uk
www.rna-uk.org

Submitting a novel

Some people submit to several editors / agents at once. Others think that this is bad form or setting yourself up for embarrassment. I've always thought that if I ever got two offers at once, I would cross that bridge when I came to it!

You need to send your submission with a stamped self-addressed envelope – unless you know that Pandora or Timothy will accept submissions by email. And record who it has gone to, and when, so that you don't embarrass yourself by sending it to the same person twice.

Mail it by normal post. If you want to be certain that it arrived safely, include a stamped self-address postcard to confirm safe receipt.

The slush pile

The phrase *the slush pile* can be uttered in a variety of tones, depending on context. It's another name for *unsolicited material*, that's all. Or it can mean *unsolicited material from authors*. As I've said elsewhere, not all publishers accept unsolicited material from authors.

Q Suzanne Jones

Is there a realistic chance of being published from the slush pile or are the odds so tiny that we should all forget our hopes of publication? Would getting an agent increase the chances of publication?

A **Tessa Shapcott**, executive editor, Modern Romance, Harlequin Mills & Boon:

There is a very realistic chance of being selected from our slush pile. We are constantly on the look-out for new authors and we know from years of success that our intake of unsolicited manuscripts will always turn up gems. We still continue to ask for a high standard of storytelling but we've never yet been disappointed: last year we acquired five new writers for Modern and Modern Heat.

We're happy to receive agented submissions. Agented and unagented submissions receive equal treatment.

www.millsandboon.co.uk

Waiting …

I'm afraid that it's a fact of life that Timothy and Pandora can take a long time to read submissions. They get a lot.

And, let's be optimistic! If they keep it for ages it might mean that your submission is being read by other people at the publisher's office or at the agency.

Try not to bug them with phone calls checking up on progress. They might just be tempted to tip your submission back into its envelope and return it, to get rid of you.

Reaction!

Sometimes, as a response to your three-chapter submission, you receive a request for the rest of the manuscript. *Woohoo!*

Don't crack open the champagne yet but congratulate yourself on the quality of your submission. It's a brilliant first step! A word of warning, though … you might be kept waiting even longer for a complete to be read than you were for the partial! But, no news is good news.

Taking revisions on the chin

After the request for the complete manuscript you might receive a phone call, email or letter to say that the editor or agent likes your work. So even if your manuscript thunks back onto your doormat one day, don't hurl it on the fire – read the letter with it. Sometimes, it's a request for revisions.

What are revisions? Oh, they just ask you to write it again …

No, not completely. The revisions (or rewrites) will normally relate to cutting out a minor character (always one you particularly love), reslanting this bit, expanding that bit or cutting something else.

If you've got this far, congratulations! Timothy is considering putting your book into an acquisitions meeting, where the editors, marketing and sales people discuss whether your book is publishable and likely to make you all some money; or Pandora thinks she might be able to sell your book to editors.

They might ask for more than one set of revisions.

Try and simply buckle down and do the work promptly and competently. If you're uncooperative now, that might be your own goose you smell cooking. Accepting and acting upon (or at least discussing) editorial direction is part of being a writer.

Rejection

Oh no! Anywhere along the process that I've described above, Timothy or Pandora might decide that they can't take your submission any further.

And your novel is rejected.

And you gaze miserably at the letter or email, unable to believe that after all that work, after all that time (a year is the longest I waited for rejection), the answer is *no*.

But remember that it's your work that's being rejected, not you. Don't take it personally. There might be any number of reasons why Pandora has said, 'No thanks!' and Timothy, 'I'll pass on this one.'

Objectively – your work *may* not be good enough. Or it may be that the subject is unpopular, not fresh enough, recently done by someone else or clashes with a sensitive political issue. Timothy may have decided the market is about to move on, Pandora that publishers aren't buying in that area. Nobody said that getting published would be easy; if it was everyone would be doing it.

If Pandora or Timothy has given you any commentary on how to improve your work, really consider what they've said. Put the book away for a while first, if need be, but think hard about whether you can use their nuggets of wisdom to make future submissions even more likely to succeed.

Whatever you do, don't allow rejections to put you off. Success may be just one submission away.

Sarah Duncan, novelist
The first time I sent out my book I got 100% rejection, the ms coming back so fast there were scorch marks down the sides of the envelope. The second time was nine months later, by which point I had completely reworked everything about my package – re-written book, new synopsis, new covering letter. I did some research and came up with a 'top six' hit-list of agents who I thought might be interested in me and what I was writing.

I sent them out on a Monday afternoon. On Wednesday morning I had the most exciting phone call of my life – an agent offering to represent me. I can remember putting the phone down, then running around the house shrieking.

Of the other submissions, I'm still waiting to hear from Agent No 2 (if you're reading this, you're a teeny bit late). I had another offer of representation and two 'nice' rejections (they liked it but …).

But it was the rejection letter from Agent No 6 that is seared into my brain. *No one wants to read depressing material like this,* she wrote. 'It's supposed to be funny,' I wailed. *Your characters are unsympathetic and one-dimensional. Worst of all: You're wasting your time, and you've just wasted mine.*

She was (and is) a well-respected agent. How could she be

wrong?

But she was, and big time.

My lovely, wonderful new agent took exactly eight days to sell the book for an advance big enough for me to give up the day job and become a full-time writer, which I've remained for the past seven years. Most readers didn't find my book depressing, my characters unsympathetic or one-dimensional and the book became my first bestseller.

It was lucky I received this rejection letter after I'd had an offer and it didn't devastate me as much as it would have done. I think if I'd had that response first or, worse, had only chosen that particular agent to send out to, I might have given up there and then. Instead I'm now published – or wasting people's time – in fourteen different countries round the world.

www.sarahduncan.co.uk

YESSSSSSSSSSSS!

You've sold the first book!

To get *the call* or *the letter* is the sweetest feeling!

Although I'd sold a lot of short stories, it was *bliss* when my agent phoned to tell me that a publisher wanted *Uphill All the Way*. I'd had a horrible afternoon running around trying to get a computer fixed, then trying to retrieve data from it that was needed the next day, then realising I'd left my mobile phone at home. I dropped in at my husband's office to ring home and tell my teenage son where I was and, over the twin soundtracks of music and the television, he said, 'Your agent phoned.'

And I lost all interest in computers and data files. 'What did she say?'

'She said for you to ring her back.'

So I did. I'm told that my side of the conversation consisted of me saying, 'You're joking! *You're joking*! YOU'RE JOKING!' And all the details of deadlines (I'd only written half the book), contracts, etc. just whooshed over my head. In fact, I had to ring her again in the morning to check that I hadn't dreamt it.

The First Rule of a successful writing career

In my experience, the First Rule of a successful writing career is never to make enemies.

You might wonder why I'm bothering you with irksome rules when we've just gone through the process of writing and selling a book. It's because that I have spoken to so many writers who haven't known about the rule. They think that now that they're *the talent* they can get their own way and if they're feeling a bit snappy they needn't hide it because they provide the material that's going to make everybody rich.

Sooner or later, each of them seems to regret not knowing the rule because the author may be *the talent* but, when you're a new author, the publisher is generally *the power*.

So, if you have a worry, put it forward politely.

If you have an objection, negotiate rather than rant.

Or let Pandora put forward the worries and the objections.

Contracts

A contract has to be thrashed out, which can be a lengthy process. If you have an agent then you'll be consulted. Pandora will advise you, present alternatives, demystify the jargon, and all you have to do is wait for the contract to arrive, complete with dotted line for you to sign on.

If you don't have an agent, I recommend that you consider getting advice.

The best way I know of is to join the Society of Authors (www.societyofauthors.org). Apart from the very many other benefits to members such as discounts on books, healthcare, insurance and accommodation, the Society has experts to vet your contracts and advise. I've used the service and it's excellent.

I was given a point-by-point commentary and recommendations, including replacement clauses where appropriate, and an invitation to ring and discuss anything I didn't understand.

It's really easy to be so glad to get a contract that you don't worry about percentages and warranties but there might be a time in the future when you do worry about those very things because you're not getting the income to which you assumed you were entitled or find you're responsible for meeting an expense you had never dreamed to be yours.

You might be with one of those publishers who offer a standard contract. I've heard it claimed that there's no such thing as a standard contract and every contract is negotiable but I've also spoken to writers who made that very point and were told that their only choices were to take it or leave it.

Standard or negotiable, it's sensible to understand everything you can about your contract and to remember, always, that First Rule of a writing career – don't make enemies. Put forward your own ideas without rubbishing theirs and support your suggestions with fact where possible.

A few main areas to be aware of:

Copyright. You should always retain the copyright in your work, which will allow for you to be paid separately for various rights and retain control.

Rights. Many publishers like to acquire all rights – in other words, they want the right to try and sell subsidiary rights, that is the right to publish in various areas of the world and in various formats. If you're one of Pandora's clients then she sees this as her job but if you don't have an agent you might like your publisher to handle all rights, although the share they take for this is rather high (check that you get more than they do). Decide whether you can sell rights yourself, whether you could get as good a deal as the publisher and whether you mind giving the time up to the task.

Royalty on cover price versus royalty on net receipts. This is one that foxes a lot of people. What is the difference? It can be quite a lot. If your royalty is 7.5% *of a cover price* it might not sound as good as 10.0% *of net receipts*. But it's better. Let's suppose for the sake of ease that your book's cover price is £10 (it probably won't be, but it's easy to work out). 7.5% of £10 is 75p. For every book sold, you get 75p. But if your royalty is based on net receipts then you only get 10.0% of what the publisher gets *after discount.* It's not unusual for publishers have to give discounts of 40-60%: £10, less discount of 60% gives £4 and 10.0% of that is only 40p. For every book sold, you get 40p. If the discount is 40% then you get 60p. Still a lot less than 75p. You can see why more and more publishers prefer to negotiate contracts based on net receipts.

Advance. As mentioned elsewhere, it's just like getting some of your wages early. An advance is likely to be payable in about three instalments, i.e. a third on signature, a third on delivery of the manuscript and a third on publication.

Multi-book deals. I haven't mentioned these until now but some publishers will ask for a contract that covers two, three or more books. So you need to be comfortable that you can deliver to the schedule. A publisher of a mainstream book of 80,000 to 120,000 words might ask for one book a year but a publisher of a shorter category romance (50,000 to 75000 words) might want two or three. They'll normally want you to supply subsequent books of a similar type to the one they've just bought – so don't think you can suddenly branch off into vampires if your first book was a sweet romance.

I really do recommend that you get the contract checked out.

More edits and revisions
What? *More!*

Afraid so. These are not a criticism of you. Don't think that your editor is regretting taking you on. It's normal for writers to have revisions after acceptance and you can expect that to be a feature of every book. You, Pandora, Timothy and all of Timothy's team, are all working with one purpose – to make the love story you wrote the most saleable love story possible. Working to make it fly off shelves and get wonderful reviews, for readers to want to be your heroine and get off with your hero. So work with it.

If you think revision requests are unreasonable or plain wrong, remember the First Rule and negotiate pleasantly. A request that has given you sleepless nights might be dismissed by an airy, 'OK! It was only a suggestion!' Or a firmer stand might be taken. But I've only ever once heard of real, insurmountable problems at this stage of the process.

Just when the manuscript is in what you think is the final form, along will come somebody called a copy editor and go through the whole thing again, word by word, checking the spelling, grammar, punctuation, continuity, good sense, flow, etc. And a good copy editor who is sympathetic to your book and your characters is a joy.

One who doesn't employ commonsense or is overzealous … not so much.

But you can normally write *stet* beside suggested changes if you don't agree with them or provide notes as to which changes you don't accept. A copy editor can cause irritation by insisting on correct grammar in dialogue rather than letting ordinary people speak like ordinary people, or wanting Alison to be Alison throughout when you want her sister to call her Ally. Don't get upset. Just ask to keep those examples as you wrote them.

But don't expect the publisher to be happy with incorrect grammar throughout just because it sounds right to you. The copy editor is paid to know the difference between commonly confused words or when to use *that* and when to use *which*. And they're good at it.

If you're not certain about how to go about making your corrections – blue pen? Red pen? In the body text? In the margin? – Timothy doesn't mind being asked for guidance.

Although lots of writers groan about checking the copy edits, it's a final opportunity to change clunky phrases and if you'd like a dedication and/or acknowledgements and your publisher hasn't mentioned them, this is a good time for you to insert them - and having copy edits is proof that you have a contract!

It will probably say, in your contract, that there's a limit to how many changes *you* can make at the copy edit stage without becoming liable for the costs. So changing a few sentences or adding people into the acknowledgements is quite acceptable. Rewriting several chapters is not.

Blurb, etc.

Some publishers ask you to write your own blurb, some editors write it for you; sometimes it's a collaborative project. I find blurb writing difficult. The synopsis was bad enough but it was, ultimately, discarded. The blurb won't be - it will be there on the jacket for the world to read.

It will appear on booksellers' websites.

You might use it on promotional material such as bookmarks, flyers, postcards or posters.

It's a powerful marketing tool.

Aim for three or four paragraphs to entice the reader in. Use powerful language appropriate to the book - if it's a tear-jerking saga you might want to use words such as *heartbroken, lost, angry*; but if you've written a feel-good romance you can avoid negative words altogether, even while letting the reader know that there are conflicts aplenty.

So, *haunted by the past* for a saga but the more encouraging *determined to face the past* for the feel good romance. Words such as *love* and *lust* will fit nicely on either!

Use hooks, introduce characters, pose questions - but never give away the ending!

If you are asked to write or collaborate upon your blurb, read as many blurbs as you can from published books that are similar to yours. A bookshop won't mind you spending an hour checking out their stock. Get a feel for what is being asked of you.

Promotion

Promotion and publicity loom large in the life of many writers. And maybe that should be *all* writers.

Writers who sell squillions of books might have help from their publishers, or even have their own publicist, but most of us don't. Or we have a little attention from a publicist at our publishers, a person who has lots of authors to promote. Take advantage of whatever is offered.

A first step will probably be for the publisher to ask you to fill in an *Author Information Sheet* and this is the opportunity for you to mention bookshops with which you might have a relationship or connection, towns that appear in the book, where you grew up, where you've lived, where you are now, any connection to a particular profession or peculiar hobby. What the publicist is looking for is an opportunity to promote you – so try and give it to them if it's there.

To augment whatever the publisher can do for you, you can use these:

Website. Yes, these can be costly but they can be free, too – just put *free website* into your search engine and you'll find loads of ways to create websites without cost and, with luck, without fuss. If you're a technophobe, consider bargaining with / bribing / paying a family teenager to do it for you. Or you might be given a page at your publisher's website. But you need somewhere for readers to make contact with you.

Blog. A blog is normally free. It took me an afternoon to set up and upload the first post but you might be quicker. I lost the damned thing twice. Decide how often you're going to post – it need not be each week or each day. Also, look out for existing blogs which have a large hit rate and offer to guest blog. Or join a blog that's run by a group so you need blog only once in a while.

Social networking sites. I'm talking about Facebook, Twitter, Bebo, Myspace, etc. Some people love these sites, some find them pointless. But they are a way of making contact with readers.

Newsletters. To reach a large audience these need to be electronic and don't need to be long. You will probably be able to allow sign-up from your website.

Promotional material such as bookmarks, cards, postcards, flyers. If you have something to give out, you'll find it easier to tell people about your book. I find bookmarks invaluable at book signings. Shoppers feel they're being given something useful and they can have a quick read of it behind the bookshelves to decide if they want to buy the book.

Press releases (PRs). Learn how to write these (there are whole books on the subject) and bombard your local radio stations and newspapers, even women's magazines. You might get interviews out of them. There are also press release websites.

Talks. Often at libraries or conferences but also at literary festivals – every town / city / village seems to have at least one literary festival where you can give a talk or a workshop on a given subject and sell your books. I know this isn't for everybody.

Book signings. Again, not for everybody. But signed books do make good presents! Shoppers are aware of this. Or can be brought to realise it!.

As so many of us have little or no experience of doing talks, I asked **Hugo Summerson,** a director of Speaker Skills Training, to give us his **Top Five Tips.**

- Carefully research your audience and the occasion. Always

do this, and allow plenty of time for it.

- When preparing your speech cover only the points that your research tells you the audience most wants to hear about. Do not spread yourself too thinly.
- Make a structure (opening – tell them what you will be talking about – main points – conclusion). Use everyday language made as vivid as possible by plentiful use of anecdote, example and illustration.
- Stick to your allotted time.
- Be enthusiastic about your subject. Enthusiasm plus preparation will help you overcome nervousness on the day.

www.speaker-skills-training.co.uk

Don't be squeamish or wussy about promo – just be selective. If you would rather grow a bunion than do a book signing, avoid it. But do look for opportunities that are your cup of tea and try to get a website, if you haven't already, because your readers are going to be very important to you.

Have a public face that is accessible to them.

Jenny Barden, writer and organiser of "Get Writing" Conference

Moments before settling down to write this piece about the merits of contributing to a literary conference, I got an email from my agent summarizing the advantages very nicely. I'd given him the line-up for the Verulam Writers' 'Get Writing' Conference (since I wanted his advice on a possible third agent to invite). 'All very impressive,' he said, 'And a good thing for your authorial profile too.' That endorsement applies just as much to speakers and workshop leaders as it does to those involved in the organizing of writers' conventions, and given an opportunity for key participation, any writer, published or aspiring, would be well-advised to take advantage.

The benefits are many-layered, direct and long-term, obvious and unseen. A billed speaker immediately gains through publicity, and the greater the marketing for the convention, then the more will be the boost given to that individual's profile. In these days of web-marketing this is particularly important. Not only do all those targeted directly as potential attendees get to hear of the speaker's billing, but anyone doing a casual internet search against that speaker's name, or for a conference of similar ilk, will find the speaker and a record of their involvement as well. This is the sort of thing that publishers love: they want to see their authors engaged in self-promotion – the higher the profile, the better the chances of selling that author's work. And the advertising can be wide-ranging: from flyers to email shots, to radio interviews and press articles; conference publicity can give those involved a tremendous uplift.

Following on from all the pre-conference advertising, there will be more direct opportunities for promotion at the conference itself. Those attending will expect a published author to refer to his or her work (though perhaps not as many times as Jeffrey Archer whom I once heard in an interview managing to mention his book or his name in just about every other sentence!). So plugging one's own work during a presentation is quite in order, and this can apply just as much to short stories and articles as to novels and books. Moreover the format of such gatherings will almost invariably include some provision for book-signing. Any published author participating would be missing a trick unless armed with copies to sign and sell (in the absence of a publicity team to do the necessary of course!).

The advantages do not end with publicity and sales; there are other benefits to taking a primary role at a literary conference. Key participation will open up the potential for making invaluable contacts and networking. Those having influence at such events are much more likely to take notice of someone who leads, and making a good impression may well reap dividends in the form of a name remembered later. The publishing world remains at heart quite self-contained and inter-connected; achieving recognition at a literary conference is one way of establishing and maintaining a useful level of integration.

Lastly, and perhaps most intangibly, there is the benefit that derives from communicating with an audience directly. To deliver a talk or manage a workshop, even to participate in a panel or organise a conference, involves some degree of self-projection and getting a message across, which in turn necessitates a consideration of what will appeal to the audience. For much of the time as writers we are locked away in splendid isolation, usually concerned more with what we want to say than with winning over our readers, but public speaking and dealing with the demands of an audience, however limited the exposure, puts the priority back on the right footing. To succeed, the writer must entertain.

Money
If you're new to the business, you might be excused for thinking that you sell your book, the publisher gives you shedloads of dosh and that's that.

Hmm. It sounds good. But …

As I said earlier, some income – often quite a proportion – comes from subsidiary rights, so you need to be aware of the need to exploit those possibilities, or talk about them to Pandora because an agent has a number of clients and it's sensible for you to keep an eye on what's happening to your work.

And there is other income due to you that you need to know how to collect.

Let's hear from **Penny Grubb**, chairman of the Authors' Licensing and Collecting Society

Once you are a published writer, one of the best things you can do is join the Authors' Licensing and Collecting Society (ALCS).

Why? There are several reasons, but let's be pragmatic to start with. Writers don't earn much. More than half those surveyed earned below the minimum wage in a 2005 study[1]. Joining ALCS will earn you an average of £300 per year and for some writers substantially more.

Where does the money come from? ALCS collects money from the secondary use of writers' work around the world, mainly photocopying, cable retransmission, private copying and public lending right, and distributes it amongst our members.

So much for the hard cash. There's a bigger picture too. Writers are an essential part of a huge creative industry. Publishing in the UK is the second largest copyright industry, topped only by software. All industries need to innovate and take risks to keep at the top of their game. The creative industries are no exception, but in other sectors, manufacturing say, large corporations take the financial risks. They budget for research and development and pay their researchers a salary while new products and technologies are developed.

Not so in our industry. Most of the financial risk taken to develop new ventures is taken individually by the multitude of creators, writers and artists, working on their own. Only a tiny number of writers are paid to develop new manuscripts, write new scripts or research new books. Instead, they put in months

---

1 What are words worth? Counting the cost of a writing career in the 21st century: a survey of 25,000 writers. Centre for Intellectual Property Policy & Management, Bournemouth University, commissioned by ALCS. 2005.

and years of effort at their own expense having no hope of a return until the work is finished and no guarantee even then. Our economy benefits enormously from creative industry and the writers who are its lifeblood deserve fair payment from those who use their work.

To receive secondary royalties after publication does not usually fill the financial gap but it makes a big difference to many writers' incomes, and secondary royalties can continue for years, long after primary royalties have dried up.

It is the collecting societies like ALCS who provide writers with income that their works have earned but that they have no means to collect individually. It is the writers' organisations and unions who give individual writers a voice, protect their copyright and maintain the flow of income that helps the creative industries to flourish.

ALCS is a not-for-profit collecting society that has paid tens of millions of pounds to writers since it was set up in 1977.

If you are a member of the Society of Authors or the Writers' Guild of Great Britain, membership of ALCS is free. If not, there is a small one-off joining fee that is taken from your first royalty payment so you pay nothing up front.

Check out the website to learn more. www.alcs.co.uk

NB Membership of the ALCS is worthwhile not just if your novel is published but for short stories or serials, too.

As well as ALCS, you'll hear writers talking about PLR (Public Lending Right). This varies from country to country but, if you live in the UK, you should register every one of your books with PLR as soon as it is published.

You can find all you need to know about PLR at www.plr.uk.com but, in essence, it's the right for authors to receive payment for the loans of their books by UK public libraries. A sample of libraries across the UK records borrowings and for every loan the writer receives a small sum. Small sums add up and a PLR payment can be thousands of pounds.

Register every print edition of every book – large print, paperback, hardback – if it's possible to borrow the edition through the UK public library system. So translated copies *can* be registered (a percentage going to the translator) but you're unlikely to get much PLR; ebooks aren't eligible at all and neither are audio books (which are rented, not borrowed). Whether writers will ever get anything from the renting of audio books is being handled by the ALCS.

If your books are published in other countries, you may get PLR from that country if there's a reciprocal agreement between it and the UK – but you need to register with the ALCS to do so.

This seems an excellent place for this question:

Q Suzanne Jones.
I know it's vulgar to ask, but is it realistic to expect to make a living from writing romantic fiction? I know there are superstars, but what about the other published writers – are they able to give up their day jobs?

A **Julie Cohen**, novelist
It's possible given hard work and some creativity, but I think you have to be flexible, realistic and prepared for times of uncertainty. I gave up my teaching job when I had my son, after having sold six books to Mills & Boon and two to Headline's Little Black Dress imprint. Because I was working full-time up till then, I saved a good amount of my advances from those eight books, so I had a safety cushion when I quit the day job.

Also, five of those books had already earned out their advances and were making me some money. I never could have quit my job if I didn't already have the savings and income, or if my husband weren't working.

Our household has taken a substantial cut in income since I gave up the day job to write. On the other hand, it's a job I can do from home and easily combine with child care, so our expenditures that way are less. If we hadn't had children, or if I were single, I would probably have kept on teaching part-time and writing full-time, because the day job would give me a stable income. Writing income can be pretty unpredictable; I know, roughly, when the royalty and advance cheques and PLR payments are coming but I can't accurately predict how much money I'll be getting and the cheques don't always turn up bang on time. Being between contracts can be pretty nerve-wracking. You hope your advances and royalties are going to go up with each new contract but life and publishing often don't work that way. Unless you're one of those superstars, writing novels tends to pay less on an hourly basis than just about any other job.

I make some extra money giving workshops, teaching courses and doing work in schools and, if I had time, would be trying to sell some journalism, too. My backup plan is to return to teaching if the writing becomes less profitable but I know I'll never stop writing whatever happens. I work very hard, but so much about this business is out of the writer's control. I count myself extremely lucky to support myself through writing fiction, because I know that many writers find it difficult.
www.julie-cohen.com

Conclusion
So, have I told you how to make money writing romantic or erotic fiction? Well, you've heard from a lot of people who do it.

Including me.

But I haven't got ready-made billion-seller plots to give you or miraculous secrets to share. It's like many other jobs – hard.

I read today that old adage that quitters don't win and winners don't quit and that's certainly a fact known to the majority of published writers. Persistence is a quality that you need in bucketloads.

Luckily, writing romantic or erotic fiction is fun. And that really helps.

I hope you enjoy it, too. And that it earns you some money.

Index

More titles in the
Secrets to Success Writing Series
from Accent Press…

9781907016196

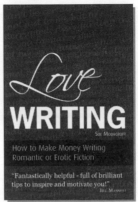

9781906373993

9781906373627

9781906125127

www.accentpress.co.uk

Successful Novel Plotting

Jean Saunders

Lost the plot? Get help with this invaluable writers' guide and in no time you'll be turning out real page-turners.

What is it about a good book that hooks the reader and makes them want more? *A good plot.*

Every best-selling author from Agatha Christie to Terry Pratchett knows the importance of a strong story.
But for the budding author it can be daunting and even confusing.

How do you turn that seed of an idea into a great epic?

This authoritative guide will help steer new writers through the minefield of the writing process.

Using examples from her own work, and that of other top authors, Jean explains how to create memorable characters, generate cliff-hangers and keep up a pace that will hook readers.

Jean Saunders is an award-winning author of more than 600 short stories and 100 novels. She's best-known as Rowena Summers, the writer of many novels based in the West Country, and Rachel Moore, author of wartime sagas set in Cornwall. Her WW1 saga Bannister Girls was short-listed for the Romantic Novel of the Year award. Jean now lectures on writing and writes a monthly column for Writing Magazine.

ISBN 978190637627 price £9.99.

The Writer's ABC Checklist

Lorraine Mace &
Maureen Vincent-Northam

An easy-to-use comprehensive guide for writers on preparing and presenting their work to agents, publishers and print media.

Regardless of the writer's level or ability, there is something extremely daunting about putting together a submission. It doesn't matter if it is for an article for a magazine, or short story for a competition, a humorous anecdote, a play or TV script, a novel or non-fiction book, *The Writer's ABC Checklist* will provide answers to questions you didn't even know you should ask.

With its A–Z format, references can be found quickly and effortlessly. Unfamiliar terms are explained and bullet points at the end of most sections provide a quick reminder of the main items covered.

This unique book is packed with writing tips and is something no aspiring writer can afford to be without.

ISBN 9781907016196 £9.99

How to Write a Pantomime

Lesley Cookman

This book clearly explains how to plan and deliver a successful, traditional pantomime script.

There are thousands of pantomimes staged throughout the world every year, most of them in Britain. Most groups, whether they be amateur drama societies, schools, Women's Institutes or Village Hall committees are constantly on the lookout for something fresh and original. This is often a matter of economics, as professional pantomimes can be costly in terms of performing rights, let alone the cost of scripts. This book is aimed at those people who take part in this increasingly popular hobby, and at the writer who wishes to write a pantomime, either for a local group, or, indeed, for mass publication.

Lesley Cookman has been writing, directing and performing in pantomime for many years. Formerly a freelance journalist, she was for a time editor of *The Call Boy*, the magazine of the British Music Hall Society, and her pantomimes have been performed not only across the British Isles, but in Australia and America. Lesley has written features, short fiction, pantomimes, a musical, a non-fiction book and is currently writing the highly acclaimed Libby Sarjeant murder mystery series for Accent Press.

ISBN 96781906125127 price £9.99

Wannabe a Writer?

Jane Wenham-Jones
Foreword by Katie Fforde

This hilarious, informative guide to getting into print is a must-have for anyone who's ever thought they've got a book in them.

Drawing on her own experiences as a novelist and journalist, **Writing Magazine's** agony aunt **Jane Wenham-Jones** takes you through the minefield of the writing process, giving advice on everything from how to avoid Writers' Bottom to what to wear to your launch party.

Including hot tips from authors, agents and publishers at the sharp end of the industry, **Wannabe a Writer?** tells you everything you ever wanted to know about the book world – and a few things you didn't...

Contributors include writers Frederick Forsyth, Ian Rankin, Jilly Cooper and Jill Mansell and publishers Harper Collins, Hodder Headline and Simon & Schuster as well as leading journalists and agents.

www.wannabeawriter.co.uk

ISBN 9781905170814 price £9.99

For more information about our books
please visit

www.accentpress.co.uk

About The Author

Sue Moorcroft writes novels, short stories, serials, articles, courses and "how to" books; she has woven together strands from all these skills to bring you *Love Writing – How To make Money Writing Romantic Or Erotic Fiction.*

She's a creative writing tutor for distance learning, residential courses and adult learning.

As a long-serving committee member of the Romantic Novelists' Association, Sue is the editor of *Loves Me, Loves Me Not*, a short-story anthology published to celebrate the association's 50th Anniversary